WHAT EVERY PRINCIPAL SHOULD KNOW ABOUT

STRATEGIC
LEADERSHIP

WHAT EVERY PRINCIPAL SHOULD KNOW ABOUT LEADERSHIP
The Seven-Book Collection

By Jeffrey Glanz

What Every Principal Should Know About Instructional Leadership

What Every Principal Should Know About Cultural Leadership

What Every Principal Should Know About Ethical and Spiritual Leadership

What Every Principal Should Know About School-Community Leadership

What Every Principal Should Know About Collaborative Leadership

What Every Principal Should Know About Operational Leadership

What Every Principal Should Know About Strategic Leadership

WHAT EVERY PRINCIPAL SHOULD KNOW ABOUT

STRATEGIC
LEADERSHIP

JEFFREY GLANZ

CORWIN PRESS
A SAGE Publications Company
Thousand Oaks, California

For information:

Corwin Press
A Sage Publications Company
2455 Teller Road
Thousand Oaks, California 91320
E-mail: order@corwinpress.com

Sage Publications Ltd.
1 Oliver's Yard
55 City Road
London EC1Y 1SP
United Kingdom

Sage Publications India Pvt. Ltd.
B-42, Panchsheel Enclave
Post Box 4109
New Delhi 110 017 India

Printed in the United States of America.

Library of Congress Cataloging-in-Publication Data

Glanz, Jeffrey.
What every principal should know about strategic leadership / Jeffrey Glanz.
    p. cm.
Includes bibliographical references and index.
ISBN 1-4129-1592-9 (pbk.)
    1. School principals—United States. 2. School management and organization—United States. 3. Strategic planning—United States. I. Title.
LB2831.93.G532 2006
371.2'012—dc22   2005021149

This book is printed on acid-free paper.

05   06   07   08   09   10   9   8   7   6   5   4   3   2   1

Acquisitions Editor:	Elizabeth Brenkus
Editorial Assistant:	Candice L. Ling
Project Editor:	Tracy Alpern
Copy Editor:	Rachel Hile Bassett
Proofreader:	Christine Dahlin
Typesetter:	C&M Digitals (P) Ltd.
Indexer:	Gloria Tierney
Cover Designer:	Rose Storey
Graphic Designer:	Scott Van Atta

Contents

*To Ronald Applbaum and Richard Guarasci, who
exhibited the very best of strategic leadership. Their ability to think and act
strategically, with vision and insight, are unparalleled. They served as role models.*

Acknowledgments

The good work we do as principals doesn't happen in a vacuum, nor does it happen by chance. Working hard and long, too, may not yield the results we desire. Organizationally aware principals realize that a plethora of ever-changing social, economic, and political conditions affect their work and workplace. Considering these external and internal influences in light of the institutional mission and then developing plans or strategies for dealing with them are constantly on the minds of strategic leaders. Principals are not concerned with maintaining the status quo; they look for ways to change and thus transform their schools. As Shirley McCune and Ronald Brandt have said, "Strategic planning is a management process for changing and transforming organizations." Principals as strategic leaders go about their work methodically by incorporating short- and long-term planning initiatives in order to improve their organization. They are forward looking, thoughtful, and intelligent, as are the readers of this volume and series. This book and series are dedicated to all who aspire to the principalship, who currently serve as principals, or who have been principals and to all who believe in such work. No nobler enterprise and profession exist, for principals are the ones who take the important time to reflect, plan, organize, manage, and strategically design educational environments and landscapes that support student learning.

* * * * * * * * * * * * * * * *

Thanks to Karyn Stevenson, former New York City public school principal and now adjunct professor at Wagner College, for sharing her experiences in strategic leadership. Thanks to Vincenza Gallassio, a principal in Staten Island, New York, who shared her expertise as well (see case study in Chapter 1). Thanks also to E. Scott Miller, local instructional superintendent in New York City, for his insights (see case study in Chapter 1) and for providing access to a sample Comprehensive Educational (Strategic) Plan that served to guide this work. Appreciation is extended to Dr. Alyce Hunter, school administrator and adjunct professor, for information about the West Morris Regional High School strategic plan discussed in Chapter 2. Thank you to editor Lizzie Brenkus for her patience, continued support, and willingness to assist me in any way to complete this project. Many thanks also go to Robb Clouse, editorial director, who prompted me to consider a trilogy of sorts: a book about teaching, which eventuated into *Teaching 101*; a book about assistant principals, which led to *The Assistant Principal's Handbook*; and a book about principals, which resulted, to my surprise, in this groundbreaking series, *What Every Principal Should Know About Leadership.*

Special thanks to my wife, Lisa, without whose support such a venture would be impossible. I love you . . . at least as much as I love writing.

Corwin Press gratefully acknowledges the contributions of the following individuals:

Randel Beaver, Superintendent
Archer City Independent School District
Archer City, TX

James Halley, Superintendent
North Kingstown School District
North Kingstown, RI

Paul Young, Executive Director, Author
West After School Center
Lancaster, OH

About the Author

 **Jeffrey Glanz, EdD**, currently serves as Dean of Graduate Programs and Chair of the Department of Education at Wagner College in Staten Island, New York. He also coordinates the educational leadership program that leads to New York State certification as a principal or assistant principal. Prior to arriving at Wagner, he served as executive assistant to the president of Kean University in Union, New Jersey. Dr. Glanz held faculty status as a tenured professor in the Department of Instruction and Educational Leadership at Kean University's College of Education. He was named Graduate Teacher of the Year in 1999 by the Student Graduate Association and was also that year's recipient of the Presidential Award for Outstanding Scholarship. He served as an administrator and teacher in the New York City public schools for 20 years. Dr. Glanz has authored, coauthored, or coedited 13 books and has more than 35 peer-reviewed article publications. With Corwin Press he coauthored the bestselling *Supervision That Improves Teaching* (2nd ed.) and *Supervision in Practice: Three Steps to Improve Teaching and Learning* and authored *The Assistant Principal's Handbook* and *Teaching 101: Classroom Strategies for the Beginning Teacher.* More recently, he coauthored *Building Effective Learning Communities: Strategies for Leadership, Learning, & Collaboration.* Most recently, Dr. Glanz has authored *What Every Principal Should Know About Leadership: The 7-Book Collection:*

What Every Principal Should Know About Instructional Leadership

What Every Principal Should Know About Cultural Leadership

What Every Principal Should Know About Ethical and Spiritual Leadership

What Every Principal Should Know About School-Community Leadership

What Every Principal Should Know About Collaborative Leadership

What Every Principal Should Know About Operational Leadership

What Every Principal Should Know About Strategic Leadership

Consult his Web site for additional information: http://www .wagner.edu/faculty/users/jglanz/web/.

* * * * * * * * * * * * * * * *

The "About the Author" information you've just glanced at (excuse the pun . . . my name? . . . Glanz, "glance"?!) is standard author bio info you find in most books. As you'll discover if you glance at . . . I mean *read* . . . the Introduction, I want this book to be user-friendly in several ways. One of the ways is that I want to write as I would converse with you in person. Therefore, I prefer in most places to use the first person, so please excuse the informality. Although we've likely never met, we really do know each other if you think about it. We share a common passion about leadership, school building leadership to be more precise. We share many similar experiences. In an experiential, almost spiritual, sense, we have much in common. What I write about directly relates, I hope, to your lived experience. The information in this volume, as with the entire series, is meant to resonate, stir, provoke, and provide ideas about principal leadership, which is vital in order to promote excellence and achievement for all.

This traditional section of a book is titled "About the Author." The first paragraph in this section tells you what I "do," not "about" me or who I am. I won't bore you with all details "about me," but I'd like just to share one bit of info that communicates more meaningfully about "me" than the information in the first paragraph. I am (I presume like you) passionate about what I do. I love to teach, guide, mentor, learn, supervise, and lead. For me, leadership is self-preservation. Personally and professionally, I strive to do my very best, to use whatever God-given leadership talents I possess to make a difference in the lives of others. I continually strive to improve myself intellectually, ethically, socially, but also physically and spiritually. I realize that I cannot lead alone. Leadership is a shared responsibility. It involves enormous commitment to excellence. We cannot achieve excellence without mindful planning. Strategic leadership is imperative.

If any of the information in this book series touches you in any way, please feel free to contact me by using my personal e-mail address: tora.dojo@verizon.net. I encourage you to share your reactions, comments, and suggestions, or simply to relate an anecdote or two, humorous or otherwise, that may serve as "information from the field" for future editions of this work, ultimately to help others. Your input is much appreciated.

Questionnaire: Before We Get Started . . .

*D*irections: Using the Likert scale below, circle the answer that best represents your on-the-spot belief about each statement. The questionnaire serves as an advanced organizer of sorts for some of the key topics in this book, although items are purposely constructed in no particular order. Discussion of each topic, though, occurs within the context of relevant chapters. Responses or views to each statement are presented in a subsection following the questionnaire (this section begins "Now, let's analyze your responses . . ."). You may or may not agree with the points made, but I hope you will be encouraged to reflect on your own views. Reflective activities follow to allow for deeper analysis. Elaboration of ideas emanating from this brief activity will occur throughout the text and series. I encourage you to share reflections (yours and mine) with colleagues. I'd appreciate your personal feedback via the e-mail address I've listed in the "About the Author" section.

SA = Strongly Agree ("For the most part, yes.")
A = Agree ("Yes, but . . .")
D = Disagree ("No, but . . .")
SD = Strongly Disagree ("For the most part, no.")

SA   A   D   SD   1. I believe that long-term planning is important but impractical, because very few of us have the time.

SA   A   D   SD   2. There's no difference between long-term planning and strategic planning.

SA   A   D   SD   3. I see little, if any, connection between action research and strategic planning.

SA   A   D   SD   4. Data-driven decision making is a laborious process that is, in reality, quite simple and has marginal value at best because of the lack of a standard form of assessment.

SA   A   D   SD   5. I never let politics interfere with my work.

SA   A   D   SD   6. Strategic leaders realize that change is inevitable and therefore plan for it.

SA   A   D   SD   7. I am committed to social justice.

SA   A   D   SD   8. Building leadership capacity and sustainability are imperative for a strategic leader.

SA   A   D   SD   9. Transformational leadership is a principal's primary responsibility.

SA   A   D   SD   10. Learning about strategic planning would be facilitated by reading a sample Strategic Plan.

Before we analyze your responses, consider the fact that our beliefs influence our actions and, more specifically, our commitment to strategic planning. Do you really believe that the time spent on short- and long-term planning makes sense, given the volatile and ever-changing nature of the educational landscape? Some might posit that principals merely need to be able to "think on their feet" and respond well to the crises that are inevitable occurrences in the life of a building principal. Principals, they might say, do not have the luxury of sitting in their offices and devising long-term plans. This book does not share these views of the dubious value of strategic planning. On the contrary, not only are such planning initiatives necessary and beneficial to the school organization, but without such efforts, the school will wallow in mediocrity, at best, and will constantly remain vulnerable to the vicissitudes of social and political forces. Still, this work does concur with the notion that in-depth planning and adhering to such plans have limitations. Principals must be prepared, indeed, to alter their plans and remain flexible enough to modify or revise them based on newly accumulated data. Such flexibility does not mitigate the value of long-term and strategic planning. Without a firm belief that such strategic work will make a difference to the school organization, a principal will not commit the time and energy it takes to actualize strategic planning. Of course, sometimes principals are not afforded the luxury of choosing to strategize; sometimes, they are compelled by local school district or state policy. Examine the premises that follow to determine your commitment to strategic work. Do the following ideas and activities match your own sense of how you see yourself involved in such work?

A strategic leader:

- considers the present social, cultural, economic, and political realities that shape a school;
- utilizes the unique talents of school faculty and staff to collaborate on planning initiatives;
- sees and envisions future possibilities for nurturing, developing, and maintaining school excellence;
- commits to visioning and possibilities for future growth and school improvement;
- thinks creatively about different ways of improving his or her school;
- conducts action research to generate ideas and to field-test possible solutions to problems;
- involves many in-school and out-of-school officials in planning initiatives;
- collects data to inform decision making;

- is willing to change course if necessary based on newly accumulated data;
- encourages innovative ideas and thinking by all members of the school community;
- connects, in purposeful ways, strategic planning to promoting student achievement.

As you consider the meaning and relevance of strategic leadership, share your thoughts about these questions with a colleague:

Reflective Questions

1. Do you really believe strategic initiatives are essential to your work as principal? How so? Be specific.

2. How much time would you devote to such strategic efforts? With all that you do, how would you find the time to strategically plan and conduct all the necessary follow-up activities involved in the process?

3. How would you go about initiating a strategic plan initiative?

4. What does strategic leadership mean to you, and why is it so important (if it is)? Explain.

5. What are specific ways you solicit school and community collaboration for your strategic initiatives?

6. What strategic practices or plans have you seen that really work well? Share with a colleague.

---

* * * * * * * * * * * * * * * *

Examine these quotations on strategic leadership. What do they mean to you?

"Thinking about and attempting to control the future are important components of planning."

—Henry Mintzberg

"One of the major differences between conventional planning and strategic planning is that conventional planning tends to be oriented toward looking at problems based on current understanding, or an inside-out mind set. Strategic planning requires an

understanding of the nature of the issue, and then finding of an appropriate response, or an outside-in mind set."

—D. J. Rowley

"Critical is the realization that a school can engage in strategic planning—but lack strategy."

—Theodore Creighton

"The effective principal is like the quarterback of a football team. She pulls together a staff that is unified on where it is going and committed to the highest performance."

—James O'Hanlon and Donald O. Clifton

"Once the change has been identified, establish short- and long-term goals and corresponding strategies. Consider the following:

- *Who will be involved in making the change? . . .*
- *Who will the change affect?*
- *How will those affected respond?"*

—Barbara L. Brock and Marilyn L. Grady

"Strategy . . . is something school leaders do before a problem arises."

—Theodore Creighton

"In the world of change leadership, every act is a political act."

—Francis M. Duffy

"[N]ot every plan is a strategic plan."

—Richard Mittenthal

* * * * * * * * * * * * * * * *

Now, let's analyze your responses to the questionnaire:

1. I believe that long-term planning is important but impractical, because very few of us have the time.

Someone once said to me, "Although long-term or strategic planning may have benefits, they're really unrealistic since there's little time. Besides, any potential benefits are outweighed by the overwhelming nature of the strategic planning process." Certainly, strategic planning may be time-consuming, but effective principals will report that the benefits outweigh any potential difficulties. The benefits described below are enumerated from the Alliance for Nonprofit Management (2003–2004a) and from McNamara (1999). Each benefit below can be readily seen in practice:

- A framework and a clearly defined direction—*Wayne Smith, principal in a midwestern suburb, reports that strategic planning is a "process that enables faculty, staff, and community to look to the future with excitement and purpose." He continues, "The process is often even more important than what we achieve in the end. As people collaborate and rally around the plan, goodwill and a culture of sharing are evident. Strategic planning gives us a framework in which to conduct our work. People feel united toward a worthy set of goals."*

- An increased level of commitment to the organization and its goals—*Rubin Kravechuck, principal in an urban school in Madison, Wisconsin, describes to members of the school board how his staff has "never really been committed to anything with any modicum of zeal. This is the first time," he continues, "that my staff demonstrates by their increased levels of participation in committee work that they have bought into the strategic goals. The school as an organization is more cohesive than ever."*

- Improved quality of services for clients and a means of measuring the service—*Noelia Quesada, principal in an urban school in San Francisco, is proud of the assessment system in place "that is so integral to our strategic initiative." She explains, "We are more attentive than ever before that we are delivering high-quality instruction to all our students. We have established as part of our plan specific learning outcomes that are measurable. We in fact collect data on an ongoing basis now and use those data to inform the decisions we make about instruction and curriculum. Furthermore, our assessment system provides a base from which progress can be measured."*

- A foundation for fund-raising development—*Zechariah Kamara, principal in a suburb of Chicago, Illinois, reports that "the strategic plan has enabled our school to apply for local and state grants in a more efficient and effective manner. Our success rate has quadrupled since we implemented our plan."*

- A process to help with crisis management—*Steve Sharkey, principal of an elementary school in Reno, Nevada, explains that "our plan enables us to deal with crises more effectively. How we respond and what resources we select reflect goals and exigencies laid out precisely in our strategic plan."*

- Ensures that the most effective use is made of the organization's resources—*Janet Kennedy, principal of a middle school in Orlando, Florida, often laments the lack of resources her school has as compared with "some other schools." "Yet," she continues, "our strategic plan helps us to better utilize existing resources because we now focus the resources we do have on key priorities and not just frivolous items that are in no way connected to our strategic goals. Such practice allows us to more equitably turn down requests for funds that would not contribute to ultimate goals."*

Lucy Spisto, principal in New York City, reacts to the criticism that planning might be too time consuming by reaffirming the importance of strategic planning. "Strategic planning is essential to my effectiveness as a principal. I cannot begin a school year without updating my plan. We find the time for what's important."

2. There's no difference between long-term planning and strategic planning.

Although often used interchangeably, a subtle and important difference exists between the two concepts. Long-term plans are often made without considering future social, political, or economic realities that require educators to alter their plans, often to an extreme degree. Strategic planning is more dynamic and flexible. Such plans are often altered to accommodate new realities. Matthews and Crow (2003) state, "Effective planning is dynamic and continuous. It occurs not as a step in the process but as an integral part of the whole process. Once the plan is established, it should be continually improved as it is implemented and results are determined" (p. 183). Strategic planning is a process that considers the fact that organizations and circumstances change and that any plan must acknowledge this reality. Such planning considers changes occurring outside the organization (long-term planning considers only internal changes) (Lunenburg & Ornstein, 2004). Long-range planning is differentiated from strategic planning, according to some authorities, in that the latter may include the former. The key difference, however, centers on the word strategy. Strategy, *according to Hax and Majluf (1996):*

1. *determines and reveals the organizational purpose in terms of long-term objectives, action programs, and resource allocation priorities;*

2. *selects the businesses the organization is in, or is to be in;*

3. *attempts to achieve a long-term sustainable advantage in each of its businesses by responding appropriately to the opportunities and threats in the firm's environment, and the strengths and weaknesses of the organization;*

4. *identifies the distinct managerial tasks at the corporate, business, and functional levels;*

5. *is a coherent, unifying, and integrative pattern of decisions;*

6. *defines the nature of the economic and non-economic contributions it intends to make to its stakeholders;*

7. *is an expression of the strategic intent of the organization;*

8. *is aimed at developing and nurturing the core competencies of the firm;*

9. *is a means for investing selectively in tangible and intangible resources to develop the capabilities that ensure a sustainable competitive advantage. (p. 14)*

3. I see little, if any, connection between action research and strategic planning.

Strategic planners utilize action research (see, e.g., Mills, 2000; Glanz, 2003) to develop goals and objectives and to assess the degree to which these goals and objectives have been implemented. In the case that follows, see how action research is used in one school to promote reflection among teachers to improve student learning. In this case, the principal decides to expand the action research initiatives to support strategic goals, as is discussed briefly after the case.

In this case study, we find Maria Rodriguez, Bill Evans, Fred Alvaro, and Martha Cunningham (names and events are fictionalized) working together on a team. Reflection is integral to professional development at International High School. Time is structured into the workweek for planned reflection. Team members are free to brainstorm ideas on a wide variety of topics. Any team member can raise a problem or concern for group reaction. During one of these "reflective" sessions, Maria was concerned about students' test scores in writing. Other members shared her concern. Statewide examinations in writing had been mandated two years earlier, and the team was concerned that preliminary data indicated students were significantly deficient in this area, especially because little attention had been paid to writing under the former administration. Team members met over the summer to decide on a curriculum plan for teaching writing, eschewing the prepackaged writing programs all too common in other schools in the city. After much research and in consultation with a prominent local university, the team decided to implement a rather well-known writing program sponsored by the university, although with significant modifications. Infusing writing in all content areas together with individual and small-group "writing consults," the team set out to make writing a priority in the fall semester. The team decided to field-test the new program with a randomly selected group of students in 10th grade and identified a comparable group of 10th graders not in the program.

Supporting the team, Eric Nadelstern, the principal at the time, provided targeted professional development and encouraged action research strategies to track program success. He encouraged teams to use action research to demonstrate the impact of teaching on student writing achievement. As part of the program, students kept detailed writing portfolios that contained writing samples over time illustrating writing maturity. Writing assessments were continuously administered. Detailed monitoring of student progress along with constructive feedback were hallmarks of the program. After the administration of the statewide writing examination in May of that academic year, team members met to assess the impact of the program on student achievement, on student writing motivation, and on the effectiveness of the teaching strategies employed by the teachers.

The chart below summarizes their findings:

Instrument	Standard	Percentage meeting	Conclusion
Standardized writing achievement test	50% above 50th percentile	65% above 50th percentile (25% improvement over previous year); only 35% of girls scored above norm	Expectation met; examine achievement of girls (interviews, etc.)
Writing portfolios	At least 50% scoring "acceptable" on portfolio rubric	55% scored "acceptable," but only 15% of girls did	Expectation met overall, but examine achievement for girls
Monthly teacher-made exams	At least 50% scoring "acceptable" on writing rubric for idea development, sentence structure, and grammar	80% scored "acceptable," but significantly less for girls	Expectation met overall, but examine achievement for girls
Student surveys	At least 80% registering satisfaction with new approach to writing	70% approval rating, but only 10% for girls	Expectation not met; further study needed

Team members analyzed the data and conducted a comparative analysis with the control group. The team shared their findings with other teams and charted a course to expand the program and address the reasons why girls did not score as well as boys.

Eric Nadelstern encouraged Maria, Bill, Fred, and Martha to reflect on the process of using action research to monitor student writing progress but also to consider how such research strategies provide evidence of the impact of their teaching on student achievement. During one brainstorming session, the dialogue went something like this:

Fred: *I felt kind of empowered using alternate means of assessment to measure student writing progress. Not relying on the standardized test alone was refreshing, even though in this case the state exams reflected our qualitative and quantitative findings.*

Martha: *I know what you mean. Using research strategies to track student progress helped me greatly to adjust my teaching approaches in the classroom. For instance, after monitoring their progress, I realized what worked and didn't work, and so I made changes.*

Bill: *Well, that may be true, but it appears we weren't sensitive or attuned to the needs of girls. Having these data alerts us to something we may not have picked up as readily or quickly.*

Martha: *You're right, Bill. I guess we first have to analyze the data more closely and perhaps collect some more information through focus groups or one-on-one interviews with some of the girls. Then we'll have to differentiate instruction to accommodate their needs and do some more action research to ascertain any improvements. [Bill nods in affirmation, as do the others.]*

Maria: *For me, this action research project provided structure to make sure I—I mean, we—reflected as we proceeded. I'm not sure I would have done so myself.*

Fred: *Yeah, we acted as a team . . . participating to solve a common problem.*

Martha: *Also important is the fact that we were always conscious of the relationship between our teaching practices and the impact they would have on student achievement.*

Eric Nadelstern [to himself]: *No need to formally observe these teachers . . . action research provided the means to encourage reflection in order to promote instructional improvement and student learning.*

The principal decides to expand the action research project to other teachers in the school. He confides to a fellow administrator:

> *I am so pleasantly surprised and gratified that this initiative worked out so well. I intend to incorporate action research to help us build our strategic goals in various areas. Clearly, as a result of this last project we need to ensure in our plan that the academic standards are being achieved by both genders. Exploring the literature on gender inequities in school will be useful. Overall, though, I intend to use action research in these ways: (a) to help determine which academic and instructional areas might need support through our strategic initiative; (b) to identify, through action research, other nonacademic areas of concern within and outside the school building; (c) to use action research as a means to assess strategic initiatives, and more. Yes, action research will come in handy as we develop and carry through on our strategic plan.*

4. Data-driven decision making is a laborious process that is, in reality, quite simple and has marginal value at best because of the lack of a standard form of assessment.

Data-driven decision making is an essential skill for school building leaders involved in strategic planning. Refinement of strategic goals and objectives is based on the quality of the data obtained. Data, for instance, may indicate student failure in acquiring literacy skills such as delivery effectiveness in oral presentations. The instructional part of the strategic plan may then be extended to include curricular modifications to support this aspect of literacy development. Ideally, data, once analyzed, may lead to teacher change in behavior, which in turn influences a change in instructional delivery, which should affect student achievement. Data-driven decision making is purposeful, if not laborious; is comprehensive and ongoing, if not simple or episodic; and has the potential to promote instructional excellence in the classroom. Data-driven decision making is most effective within a larger strategic initiative.

Data-driven decision making, however, does not often represent best practice (see, e.g., Kerr, Marsh, & Ikemoto, 2005; Wayman, Midgley, & Stringfield, 2005; V. M. Young, 2005). Simply collecting data does not mean it will be used or used properly. Teachers and principals need training and experience in data collection, analysis, and interpretation as well as how to draw conclusions that will effect changes in classroom practices. As Wayman et al. (2005) have stated, "To read policy and news accounts, one might surmise that the mere act of providing student data is sufficient to create a school culture driven by this data." They continue, "On the contrary, although many educators embrace the notion of becoming more reflective practitioners, few educators have the preparatory background to engage in such analysis and reflection" (p. 2).

For data-driven decision making to have a chance of working, you as principal must provide systemic support that includes, among other areas:

- *Fundamental belief and vision in results-oriented leadership*
- *Establishment of a school culture that supports data collection, analysis, and use of data to promote student learning*
- *Availability of technological and other resources that facilitate continuous data-driven decision making*
- *Involvement of diverse internal and external community members in the process*
- *Implementation of meaningful and ongoing professional development so that educators develop the important skills of data collection, analysis, and use*

5. I never let politics interfere with my work.

"I try to avoid politics at all costs, even though I realize it's a reality of my work" may appear to be an astute comment, yet it's shortsighted, because as principal you cannot avoid the political arena. However, one traditional approach to leadership that characterized the 19th and 20th centuries was an avoidance of politics. Removing corrupt politicians from school governance was the mainstay of early school reformers (see, e.g., Glanz, 1991; Tyack, 1974). It was an appropriate focus at the time, but even after its usefulness had waned, vestiges of such an apolitical frame of reference existed throughout much of the last century. The term politics *today refers to the influence of various vested interests, groups, or individuals who wish to put forth a particular agenda. Your work as principal inevitably involves interacting with various parties who hold a particular viewpoint and wish to influence some aspect of the school as an organization. Principals today must be equipped to confront political realities and utilize them as agents to create more effective schools.*

First, you must think politically. Asking yourself, "What vested interest does this group or individual have?" does not mean you are suspicious but rather indicates your recognition of the need to fully understand a particular perspective in order to make some sort of informed decision. Drawing on Bolman and Deal's (1991) five political propositions, you should be aware of the following:

- *Schools should be viewed as "coalitions" composed of individuals and groups with vested interests.*
- *People of varied backgrounds and experiences hold "enduring differences" that include their beliefs, attitudes, dispositions, values, and perceptions, and understanding these differences is critical to strategic leadership.*
- *Deciding how to distribute and who receives the scarce resources of the school organization will take up much time and possibly lead to disagreements and dissatisfaction.*
- *"Conflict" is a reality. Conflict resolution techniques may help, but they are no panacea; "power" is vested in the principalship, as it is in various other school positions, to varying degrees.*
- *Bargaining, negotiation, and "jockeying for position" are commonplace in school organizations.*

Principals as politicians, then, think about coalitions; enduring differences; allocation of scarce resources; conflict and power; and bargaining, negotiation, and jockeying for position. Understanding power in its various forms is critical to our success as principals. As principal, you can draw on five types of power that are reviewed by Matthews and Crow (2003, citing French & Raven, 1959). As principal, you wield the following types of power:

- *The power to dispense rewards (e.g., "I am going to give you released time to attend that conference.")*
- *The power to coerce individuals or groups (e.g., "If you don't attend the meeting next week I will not release you to attend the conference next month.")*
- *Legitimate power, by virtue of the position you hold (e.g., "I want you to do this because I am the principal.")*
- *Referent power, by virtue of identifying with someone who has greater power (e.g., "The superintendent wants me to ask you to attend the conference.")*
- *Expertise power, which works because you have specialized knowledge that is respected by others (e.g., "I will attend the conference because Ms. Beyerback, the principal, is such an authority in special education, and she highly recommends this conference.")*

Politics need not be seen as a dirty word. Effective principals do not fear politics. Rather, they understand its role in schools. Blase (1991, as cited by Matthews & Crow, 2003) identifies certain characteristics of ineffective political leaders: "authoritarian, inaccessible, unsupportive, inequitable, inflexible, and inconsistent and . . . known to avoid conflict" (p. 214).

6. Strategic leaders realize that change is inevitable and therefore plan for it.

We certainly realize that change is inevitable, yet the nature and direction of change are not always easy to anticipate. Effective strategic leaders are very much aware that their plans are tentative and must remain flexible to adapt to unforeseen circumstances. Concrete strategies are provided in more detail later in this volume.

7. I am committed to social justice.

Strategic planning is not a simple technique or strategy that a principal employs to accomplish a particular objective. It emerges from a deep commitment to improve schooling and the experiences students have in them. Therefore, principals, like all educators, must affirm a commitment to the highest ideals of education so that all students, regardless of background or ability, can achieve their potential in an atmosphere of support, opportunity, and justice.

Principals affirm the following four notions that form four basic purposes of education (i.e., why we are in the business we are in). We help students achieve:

1. *Self-Realization—Included in this broad category are ideas such as striving for intellectual growth, aesthetic interests, personal development, character building, self-worth, and so forth.*

2. *Human Relationships—Included in this broad category are ideas such as developing friendships, respecting others, fostering cooperation, developing ethical and moral reasoning, promoting democracy, and so on.*

3. *Economic Efficiency—Included in this broad category are ideas such as work, career, money, consumer education, and so forth.*

4. *Civic Responsibility—Included in this broad category are ideas such as seeking social justice, exhibiting tolerance for others, promoting world peace, respecting law and order, fulfilling obligations to government, and so on.*

Education is conceived as the deliberate, systematic, and sustained effort to transmit knowledge, skills, and values that a society deems worthy (see, e.g., Cremin, 1966). Schooling represents a small part in one's overall education. Life indeed educates. You may walk down the street one morning and meet a friend who "educates" you about a specific matter. Museums, TV, family, religious institutions, theaters, libraries, salespeople, and prisons educate. Schools certainly play a vital role in education. Three purposes can be identified: (a) helping children acquire knowledge and skills; (b) transmitting ideals and values of society; and (c) preparing children to live creative, humane, and sensitive lives.

We, as principals, encourage teachers to ask the question, "Who are the students in my class, and what impacts do race, gender, and social class have on their academic, social, and emotional development?" We know that race matters, as do gender and class. Students' backgrounds and the way they have been treated by society as a result influence their behavior. Have we as a society used race, gender, and class to classify and stigmatize our students? In an effort to promote a sense of justice, we might ask the following questions:

1. *What ways might teachers either overtly or unintentionally discriminate in their classrooms?*

2. *What ways might schools either overtly or unintentionally discriminate?*

3. *How might we as principals contribute to inequities, albeit unintentionally?*

4. *What are some prejudices we might have about some people or groups, and how might they affect our interaction with them?*

5. *What groups or individuals might be targeted for discrimination?*

6. *What are some ways we might promote equality, opportunity, and justice?*

7. *What are some ways society might promote equality, opportunity, and justice, and what role can we play as transformative principal leaders?*

8. Building leadership capacity and sustainability are imperative for a strategic leader.

Strategic leaders always have the big picture in mind; they look to the future and consider an array of factors or forces that may influence the school. Strategic leaders also realize they cannot do it alone. They need to encourage others to participate in building the academic and social climate of the school. They realize that strategic goals transcend their duration in office. As such, as principal you know you must build leadership capacity (i.e., involve others in carrying out the school vision and mission) and leadership sustainability (i.e., ensuring reform efforts last over time, even beyond your term as principal).

Leader capacity, according to Lambert (1998) includes five assumptions:

- *Leadership is a reciprocal learning process that enables participants "to construct and negotiate meanings leading to a shared purpose of schooling."*
- *Leadership is "about learning that leads to constructive change" that involves the many.*

- *"Leading is skilled and complicated work that every member of the school community can learn." Lambert adds that members of the school community have the right to "actively participate in the decisions that affect their lives."*
- *"Leadership," put simply, "is a shared endeavor."*
- *If leadership is to be truly shared, then principals must build capacity by redistributing "power and authority" within the school to allow for the meaningful participation of the many. (p. 9)*

Strategic leaders also understand fully the importance of sustainability and institutionalization of reform (see, e.g., Datnow, 2005). As principal, you work hard to ensure that the innovative practices you and the school community have established will last. To do so, you would frame the strategic plan as a "live" document, not one that sits on the shelf after being signed. The plan is a guide and is meant to be revisited. You would establish structural support mechanisms (e.g., revision of lockstep class periods to, perhaps, block scheduling), procedural activities (e.g., revising standard operating procedures to accommodate the new changes), and cultural norms (e.g., provide forums for discussion of beliefs and values of school community members).

9. Transformational leadership is a principal's primary responsibility.

Transformational leadership has received much attention in the educational leadership literature (see, e.g., Leithwood & Jantzi, 2005). Although transformational leadership has been examined by other theorists (e.g., Bass, 1997; Burns, 1978), Kenneth Leithwood and Doris Jantzi have more recently addressed implications of transformational leadership for schools. According to the authors (Leithwood & Jantzi), "three broad categories of leadership practices" can be identified: setting directions, developing people, and redesigning the organization. The authors explain that setting directions is a "critical aspect of transformational leadership . . . [by] helping staff to develop shared understandings about the school and its activities as well as the goals that undergird a sense of purpose or vision" (pp. 38–39). They explain that people are more apt to participate when they have had a say in developing ideas and practices. Transformational leaders realize that anyone can set a direction for an organization, but it is the effective leader who considers and solicits the participation of other key school personnel to share in the development and actualization of the institutional vision and purpose.

Transformational leadership also involves marshalling others beyond the initial stages of school transformation. Organizations will not improve and move forward without the active and purposeful involvement of many key individuals. Effective principals as transformative leaders are people oriented and know how to motivate them. More important, they truly respect teachers and other school personnel. They discover the unique talents of each individual and suggest ways that each one can contribute meaningfully to the school mission and vision.

Redesigning the school organization is the result of setting directions for the school and the collective contribution of people in the organization. As transformative principal leader you aim to establish, nurture, and support a learning community environment in which high achievement for all students is encouraged (e.g., Sullivan & Glanz, 2006). Effective transformational leadership must be intimately connected to promoting student achievement by nurturing and personifying knowledge, skills, and dispositions that promote student achievement.

Transformational leadership is also concerned about the creation and use of knowledge by leaders to accomplish their objectives for high achievement for all students. Michael Fullan (2003a, citing Brown & Duguid, 2000) has culled ideas about a knowledge community and created a list of Brown and Duguid's beliefs about the effective use of knowledge:

- *Knowledge lies less in its databases than in its people. (p. 121)*
- *For all information's independence and extent, it is people, in their communities, organizations, and institutions, who ultimately decide what it all means and why it matters. (p. 18)*
- *A viable system must embrace not just the technical system but also the social system—the people, organizations, and institutions involved. (p. 60)*
- *Knowledge is something we digest rather than merely hold. It entails the knower's understanding and having some degree of commitment. (p. 120)*

Learning communities are clearly not unique to the world of education. Gladwell's (2000) prescription for changing people's beliefs and behavior is completely consistent with the current educational thoughts about schools:

To bring about a fundamental change . . . that would persist and serve as an example to others, you need to create a community around them, where these new beliefs could be practiced, expressed and nurtured. (p. 173)

Envisioned change will not happen or will not be fruitful until people look beyond the simplicities of information and individuals to the complexities of learning, knowledge, judgment, communities, organizations, and institutions. (p. 213)

Transformational leaders, in the end, are concerned with changing schools through democratic processes of collaboration:

Democratic schools in postmodern times require stronger leadership than traditional, top down, autocratic institutions. The nature of that leadership, however, is markedly different, replacing the need to control with the desire to support. Ironically, such leaders exercise much more influence where it counts, creating dynamic relationships between teachers and students in the classroom and resulting in high standards of academic achievement. (Nadelstern, Price, & Listhaus, 2000, p. 275)

10. Learning about strategic planning would be facilitated by reading a sample Strategic Plan.

I think so. Although plans may vary greatly, the sample below incorporates some of the essential components. Please note that some plans are quite concise, whereas others are lengthy. The plan below is culled from a rather lengthy document. I have tried to excerpt only certain parts in order to give you a sense of strategic planning. Your superintendent or district may require a different format. Many thanks go to E. Scott Miller, local instructional superintendent, and Karina A. Constantino, principal, who gave permission to use this plan. Read the plan, and answer the guiding questions that follow. The plan was signed and approved by the following constituents: team chairperson, principal, union leader, parents' association president, a student representative, the local instructional superintendent, the community school district superintendent, the regional superintendent, seven School Leadership Team teacher members, and seven School Leadership Team parent members.

Purpose of the Comprehensive Educational Plan

All school planning requires a systematic review and careful analysis of student needs and existing activities to determine how instructional areas can be improved. The process of developing the Comprehensive Educational Plan (CEP) allows School Leadership Teams an opportunity to access the effectiveness of the current instructional programs; discuss proposed modifications and alternatives; develop goals and objectives; and create action plans that will translate into observable, effective strategies to improve student achievement. These strategies must include effective, scientifically based methods for the delivery of high services (Academic Intervention Services [AIS]) for students who score below the State-designated performance level on State assessments or who are at risk of not achieving the State standards. Lastly, the School Leadership Team is asked to develop a mechanism to assess whether the proposed activities have resulted in improved student performance.

This plan should be a product of the collaborative decisions of all stakeholders: parents, staff, administrators, and students (if appropriate). Once the CEP is approved, it will serve as a focus for implementing instructional strategies, professional development opportunities, and parent involvement activities for the 2004–2005 school year.

The accompanying Guide to Completing the School CEP 2004–2005 will assist School Leadership Teams through each step of this very important process.

PLAN OUTLINE

SCHOOL INFORMATION

SCHOOL LEADERSHIP TEAM SIGNATURE PAGE

PART I: SCHOOL VISION/MISSION STATEMENT

PART II: NARRATIVE DESCRIPTION OF THE SCHOOL

PART III: SCHOOL DEMOGRAPHIC DATA

PART IV: NEEDS ASSESSMENT—SECTIONS A, B, AND C

- **SECTION A—ANALYSIS OF STUDENT ACHIEVEMENT AND PROGRAM EFFECTIVENESS**
- **SECTION B—PROCESS FOR REPORTING NEEDS ASSESSMENT FINDINGS**
- **SECTION C—IDENTIFIED PRIORITIES FOR SCHOOL YEAR 2004–2005**

PART V: SCHOOL GOALS AND OBJECTIVES

- **SECTION A—ENGLISH LANGUAGE ARTS**
- **SECTION B—NATIVE LANGUAGE ARTS**
- **SECTION J—PARENT INVOLVEMENT**
- **SECTION K—PROFESSIONAL DEVELOPMENT**
- **SECTION M—OTHER IDENTIFIED AREAS**

PART VI: ACTION PLAN

APPENDIX 1: ACADEMIC INTERVENTION SERVICES (AIS)—FOR ALL STUDENTS

APPENDIX 2: NO CHILD LEFT BEHIND (NCLB)/STATE EDUCATION DEPARTMENT (SED) REQUIREMENTS FOR SCHOOLS IDENTIFIED FOR SCHOOL IMPROVEMENT

[Including Title I Schools in Need Improvement (SINI)—Year 1 and Year 2, Title I Corrective Action (CA)

Schools—Year 1 and Year 2, NCB Restructuring Schools, Schools Under Registration Review (SURR), and

Schools Requiring Academic Progress (SRAP)]

APPENDIX 3: NCLB REQUIREMENTS FOR TITLE I SCHOOL-WIDE PROGRAMS SCHOOLS

APPENDIX 4: REVIEW TEAM RECOMMENDATIONS—FOR SCHOOLS UNDER REGISTRATION REVIEW (SURR)

Note: All schools must complete Appendix 1. All schools identified under NCLB or SED for School Improvement [including Title I Schools in Need of Improvement (SINI)—Year 1 and Year 2, Title I Corrective Action (CA) Schools—Year 1 and Year 2, NCLB Restructuring Schools, Schools Under Registration Review (SURR), and Schools Requiring Academic Programs (SRAP)] must complete Appendix 2. All Title I Schoolwide Program schools must complete Appendix 3. All SURR schools must complete Appendix 4.

Part I: School Vision and Mission—State the vision for your school community and your school's mission, which reflects its intent to achieve this vision. (*Note:* The school's vision and mission must articulate high expectations for all students.)

Vision

Our vision is to create a community of lifelong learners. The staff strives to help each child reach his or her highest potential through collaboration, congeniality, and collegiality. Through standards-based, data-driven instruction, we hope to move each child to a higher level. We will foster high academic skills for all our students. We believe that every person and every contribution, no matter how small, can create positive change. Every obstacle must be looked upon as a challenge, and every challenge, when met and overcome, builds self-esteem and confidence. This will, in turn, develop lifelong skills to make correct choices while developing self-respect.

Mission

We are a diverse, multicultural collaborative school community dedicated to achieving high academic standards for all of our students. Through high-quality, standards-driven instruction; a nurturing environment; and the development of civic, social, and technological skills, we will create a community of lifelong learners.

Because many of our children are English-language learners (ELL), the arts will become our universal language, which will weave a common thread throughout our curriculum.

Part II: Narrative Description of the School—The narrative description should provide a "snapshot" of the school and contain an accurate overview of the school's current educational program and the significant changes that will be implemented for the 2004–2005 school year. It *must* contain the following:

- Contextual information about the school's community and its unique or important characteristics
- Student achievement trends

- An overview of instructional programs and schoolwide educational initiatives, including accelerated or enriched curriculum offerings, programs for ELL students, Academic Intervention Services, and implementation of the New Continuum (for schools that are implementing the citywide programs in this narrative as well as additional school-based initiatives)
- If applicable, an overview of focused intervention(s) to address the needs of specific student subgroups that have not met the Annual Measurable Objective, the Safe Harbor target, or the 95% participation rate requirement
- Funding resources
- A detailed description of existing collaborations with community-based organizations, universities, and corporations

Narrative Description of the School

Public School 22 is a large, multicultural elementary school in the Graniteville section of Staten Island, New York. The prekindergarten through fifth-grade school serves a population of approximately 1,204 students from culturally diverse backgrounds. The community is home to many new immigrants from Mexico, Nigeria, and the Middle East. The school building consists of an old wing, which was built in the early 1900s. This part of the building houses the Early Childhood Academy, prekindergarten through grade 2. The new wing houses our middle school, which consists of grades 3 through 5. The halls are filled with students' work and accomplishments. As you walk through this busy building, you can feel the enthusiasm and excitement for learning.

According to the latest available ethnic data, 27.6% of the students are white, 24.6% are black, 35.9% are Hispanic, and 10.8% are Asian/Middle Eastern.

Approximately 7.4% of the children have Individualized Educational Plans (IEPs) and receive the full continuum of services. These services consist of Special Education Teacher Support Services, integrated inclusion classes, instruction in self-contained classes (MIS I), and related services such as speech and language therapy, counseling, and adaptive physical education. Some students also receive occupational therapy. Additionally, 5.3% of the students are ELLs, with Spanish as the dominant language among the vast majority. The proportion of children who qualify for free lunch is 56.3%.

The school houses one prekindergarten class; nine kindergarten classes, one of which is an English as a second language (ESL) class; eight first-grade classes; seven second-grade classes; nine third-grade classes; seven fourth-grade classes; and seven fifth-grade classes in general education. We also have two self-contained special education classes, one for grades 3–4 and the other class serving grades 4–5. The average class size in kindergarten is 20.9 students. Grades 1 through 3 average about 23 students, and grades 4 and 5 average 26 students. With the exception of kindergarten, children are homogeneously grouped. In the 2004–2005 school year, all students will be heterogeneously grouped from kindergarten through fifth grade. Current strategies for implementing the New Continuum include an inclusion model from District 75 with 10 children in grades kindergarten through 5. There are three push-in resource room teachers, one special ed guidance counselor, a part-time School Assessment Team, and a part-time bilingual psychologist and social worker who conduct Annual Reviews and Triennials of IEPs, two full-time speech teachers, and one part-time speech teacher. All of the above cooperate with the classroom teachers to meet the individual needs of the children. There are three full-time and two part-time Academic Intervention teachers serving grades 2 through 5. They push in to provide differentiated instruction.

The student body is served by 1 principal, 2 assistant principals, 50 classroom teachers, 10 cluster teachers, 2 guidance counselors, 5 paraprofessionals, 3.6 secretaries, 1 school safety officer, 9 school aides, 1 family associate, and 12 additional support personnel (which includes AIS teachers, speech, resources room, math and literacy coaches, ESL, two F-status teachers to support the school's programs, and a part-time speech teacher). Of the 72 teachers on staff, 100% are fully licensed and certified; 71.9% have master's degrees, and 50% have been teaching for more than five years. There are 14 first-year teachers, and 24 teachers have fewer than three years of teaching experience. With the implementation of the citywide program for literacy and math, the staff now includes full-time literacy and math coaches and a parent coordinator.

Summary of Data for the Implications for Instruction (only K–2 data are provided here)

Kindergarten

Students exhibited growth in phonemic awareness and writing skills. They also began to demonstrate reasoning ability in math with a capacity in number recognition. The need was apparent in inference-making skills and drawing conclusions in the areas of both language arts and math.

This indicates that a continued effort in differentiated instruction driven by need, combined with full classroom instructional strategies, is warranted.

Grade 1

Current first-grade teachers have articulated the need for more phonemic awareness and practice in reinforcing the skills involved with this instruction for our new first-grade pupils. The phonics curriculum that the Department of Education is initiating assists in addressing this concern, but more is needed. Students will also require additional assistance in reading comprehension skills. Teachers have expressed their belief that more instructional time should be devoted to instruction in specific skills such as inference making, drawing conclusions, determining main ideas, and utilizing contextual clues. Utilizing best practices in differentiated instruction should enable the needs of the future first grades to be met.

Writing skills will also need to be addressed. This need can be fulfilled by continuing staff development in preparing our early childhood grades with skills necessary to achieve proficiency on the fourth-grade English Language Assessment (ELA) test.

As a springboard to the upper grades, students should also be exposed to instructional activities that encourage listening skills. This can be further achieved through modeling of lessons and additional modeling of exemplary student work.

Student population is ever increasing in PS 22's ELL and Special Education categories. The school meets the needs of its ELL population with a push-in/pull-out ELL teacher for instruction of our ELL students in grades K–5. In addition, there is an ELL kindergarten classroom to address the high number of ELL students in kindergarten. The ELL teacher also pushes in to the kindergarten, including the ELL class, in a team teaching approach.

The school houses two MIS I classes for learning-disabled children in addition to three resource room teachers. One of the resource room teachers is trained in the Wilson Method for teaching reading and uses this approach with many of our at-risk children as well as with those children receiving IEP services. PS 22 hosts a full inclusion model in grades K–5. PS 373 provides 5 paraprofessionals for 10 inclusion children in attendance in grades K–5 at PS 22. There is also an onsite resource teacher to assist regular education teachers and provide them with professional development where needed. The additional paraprofessionals provide at-risk services to regular education children as well.

The needs of all children will be addressed through articulation sessions with classroom teachers and support personnel.

The AUSSIE (one of a group of Balanced Literacy specialists from Australia hired by the New York City Department of Education) focuses on grade 1 in developing read-aloud, shared reading, independent reading, guided reading, and the integration of writing throughout the curriculum. Professional development will include incorporating technical skills in the writing block during editing.

Everyday math is being implemented in first grade. The need exists, according to the assessments, to strengthen skills across the board, but particularly in data, chance, and geometry.

Grade 2

Current second-grade teachers have articulated the need to provide differentiated learning experiences for the students. This can be achieved by utilizing the different forms of assessment to drive instruction in the areas of reading comprehension, writing, and content area skills. The curriculum that is being initiated by the Department of Education assists in addressing this concern within the Literacy Block.

Teachers hope to address the development of writing skills by continuing staff development with their colleagues in the upper grades. Students should be exposed to instructional activities that encourage their listening skills. Second-grade instruction will build further on first-grade literacy activities and will further prepare the students for eventual proficiency on the fourth-grade ELA.

Everyday math is being implemented in the second grade, and the math coach works extensively with the teachers. The needs assessment shows more is needed across all skills, particularly in numeration.

School Climate

In order to foster an environment that supports learning, given the large population of the building, the need exists for a third assistant principal. This would allow a more in-depth concentration on improving instruction in each classroom. This would also allow our conflict resolution program, "Resolving Conflicts Creatively," to support a positive climate for learning to take place.

Our strong arts program in music, art, and drama weaves its way through the literacy and math block and has become the universal language for our many Hispanic and Middle Eastern children. Our population recognizes that each child has a unique gift and is a constant source of celebration. It is seen in our hallways and throughout our very large building. The chorus has been invited to perform for the Mayor and various Staten Island elected officials, as well as community organizations such as Project Hospitality and the Staten Island Zoo.

Our school is recognized by the number of grants that our teachers bring into the building, and the enthusiasm has gone beyond our borough. Paine Webber awarded our school $15,000 for a new sound system. The school placed first in the city for its projects in Team Up to Clean UP and Trashmasters—integrating science, music, and art in the literacy and math blocks.

School Utilization

The building is overutilized, and there is a constant need for creative use of space. Our school has an outdoor children's garden for special events to free up our auditorium space. We use push-in models to lower class size and for differentiated instruction. Our teachers also team-teach. We will continue to do this in the 2004–2005 school year.

Community Collaborations

PS 22 has been able to collaboratively and effectively restructure its educational programs through the following:

- AUSSIE
- Staten Island Medical Health reading volunteers
- YMCA of Greater New York (a nationally accredited after-school program)
- Free passes from the Staten Island Zoo for parents and children
- Free visit from the American Society for the Prevention of Cruelty to Animals (ASPCA) for visitations to four first-grade classes—funded through last year's Penny Harvest funds
- Free assembly from United Nations Children's Fund (UNICEF) for the fourth- and fifth-grade students—funded through last year's Penny Harvest funds
- Council of Arts and Humanities of Staten Island/Staten Island Savings Bank, which funded a grant of $2,800 for "Science Meets the Arts"—Bobaloo for three visits to each kindergarten and first-grade classroom
- Free Prejudice Reduction Program for five classroom visits to each second-grade classroom
- Free in-school and at-site (Snug Harbor) art lessons for four fourth-grade classes
- Free antismoking assemblies through the American Cancer Society for the fourth- and fifth-grade classes—funded through this year's Penny Harvest funds
- Free Project Liberty Arts residency through Marquis Studios for four third-grade classes
- Using the Trashmaster funds, Music for Many Inc. supplied a storyteller for kindergarten and first grade and African dance program for grades 2 through 5
- Penny Harvest—Common Cents
- Fresh Air Fund (2003, 2004)
- St. Georgine School
- City Harvest
- American Cancer Society (2001, 2003, 2004)

- ASPCA (2003, 2004)
- Beautification of PS 22
- Student Community Action grant—$450, which was matched by Shoprite for $500 for the soldiers at Walter Reed Hospital
- Free Fire Safety Program through Assemblyman Lavelle's office for the third-grade students
- A $3,000 grant from Parents as Arts Partners to provide parent-child trips to Blue Heron Park, Alice Austen House, Clay Pit Pond, and Wolfe's Pond Park

This year, we will continue to contract with AUSSIE to model Balanced Literacy. This year the AUSSIE's focus will be in grade 2. She will also provide staff development and will be assisted by the literacy coach, who provides modeling and staff development in grades 3 through 5. Month by Month Phonics, Voyager, and Passport are used in kindergarten through grade 5 for further assessment by both the literacy coach and the AUSSIE. This year we will introduce the Diagnostic Reading Assessment tool in each classroom from kindergarten through fifth grade.

All professional development personnel are assisting the staff in utilizing the workshop model across the curriculum content areas.

There will be an Academic Intervention teacher servicing each grade in reading and in math. The Academic Intervention teachers will also provide training for the teachers in utilizing the various assessments to drive their instruction.

The Instructional Team will continue to meet weekly and revisit all Academic Interventions to improve academic success at PS 22.

As a Title I Schoolwide Project school, all of the students will benefit from the support services offered.

Needs Assessments

Children: Diagnostic Reading Assessment

Benchmark testing in Everyday Math

Voyager

Passport

Grow Report

Early Childhood Literacy Assessment System (ECLAS)

Early Performance Assessment in Language Arts (EPAL)

Continental Press

Princeton Review (see attached grade summaries)

Running records

Portfolios

Guided Reading records

Conferencing with children in reading and math

Item Skills Analysis—available from standardized testing from the previous year

Part III: School Demographic Data—Use demographic data to provide profile of the school. (Most information can be found in school report card.)

	Percentage or Number
Student Information	
Grades served	7
Enrollment (total number of students served)	1,197
Student stability (% of enrollment)	92.5%
Attendance rate (% of days students attended)	92.9%
Suspensions (number per 1,000 students)	26.9%
Percentage of economically disadvantaged/ low-income students (eligible for free lunch)	56.3%
Number of general education students	1,102
Total number of students with disabilities (receiving IEP-mandated services)	95
Number of self-contained special education classes (for high schools: total number, in all subject areas, of special education self-contained classes)	2
Number of students in general education classes receiving IEP-mandated services	77
Number of special education students decertified this year	10
Percentage of recent immigrants	5.3%
Number of ELL and limited English proficiency (LEP) students	80
Number of bilingual classes	0
Total number of students receiving ESL services	80
Number of ELL/LEP students identified for special education	2
Percentage of ELL/LEP students attaining English proficiency	1.5%
Number of general education preschool students	36
Number of special education preschool students	0
Number of students in temporary housing	0
Ethnic and gender data (% of enrollment)	
White	27.06%

(Continued)

	Percentage or Number
Black	24.6%
Hispanic	36.9%
Asian and others (includes Pacific Islanders, Alaskan Natives, and Native Americans)	10.8%
Male	52.7%
Female	47.3%
Staff Information	
Total number of teachers	72
Percentage of teachers fully licensed and permanently assigned to the school	95%
Percentage of teachers with more than two years' teaching experience in this school	68%
Percentage of teachers with more than five years' teaching experience anywhere	53.4%
Percentage of teachers with master's degree or higher	65%
Average number of days absent	6
Number of administrative and instructional supervisors	3
Number of guidance counselors	2
Number of school psychologists	2
Number of social workers	1
Number of educational evaluators	0
Number of speech therapists	2.4
Number of occupational therapists	1
Number of physical therapists	1
Number of school nurses	2
Number of paraprofessionals providing instructional services	2
Number of paraprofessionals providing noninstructional services (i.e., health, translation, parent involvement)	3
Number of family assistants	1
Number of school aides	9
Number of school safety agents	1

Part IV: Needs Assessment—Sections A, B, and C

Part IV—Section A: Analysis of Student Achievement and Program Effectiveness—Conduct a comprehensive review and analysis of student achievement data (both schoolwide and disaggregated by each of the following student subgroups:[1] general education; ELL/LEP students; students with disabilities; economically disadvantaged students; and students from major ethnic and racial groups, including white, black, Hispanic, Asian or Pacific Islander, and American Indian/Alaskan Native, in the areas of English language arts (including ESL, where applicable), native language arts, mathematics, science, social studies, foreign language (middle and high schools), the arts, and career and technical subjects (for high schools). For each academic area, evaluate the effectiveness of curriculum and instruction (including the provision of AIS), use of technology, library media services, and professional development. In addition, assess the impact of other areas related to student achievement (i.e., student attendance, student support services, parent involvement, school climate, and school facilities). Indicate major findings and implications for instructional programs. (*Note:* For schools implementing the citywide programs for literacy and mathematics, implications should relate to individualized strategies for the effective implementation of instructional programs to meet school-specific student needs.)

Part IV—Section A.1: Analysis of Student Achievement

1. Early Childhood Grades (Prekindergarten through grade 2)

Data Analysis/Findings—Early Childhood

Students exhibited growth in phonemic awareness and writing skills. They also began to demonstrate reasoning ability. The need was apparent for inference-making skills and drawing conclusions in language arts and math. The data used to determine this included the early childhood literacy assessment system, student portfolios, and teacher observation. An Academic Intervention teacher will provide early intervention.

Current first-grade teachers have articulated the need for more phonemic awareness and practice in reinforcing the skills involved with this instruction for our new first-grade pupils. Students will also require additional assistance in reading comprehension skills as well as writing skills. The reading recovery teacher will provide Academic Intervention in grade 1.

In the second grade, the teachers have articulated the need to provide differentiated learning experiences for the students, who come in with such varied needs. During professional development, teachers will be provided with the strategies to achieve this goal through technology and literacy development.

---

1. For all students, disaggregated student achievement data are available in the areas of English language arts and mathematics for each of the listed student subgroups. Disaggregated student achievement data for science are also available for elementary and middle schools.

Implications for the Instructional Program

In kindergarten, a continued effort in differentiated instruction driven by need with full-classroom instructional strategies is warranted.

[*Note:* The next page, not excerpted, includes a summary of statistics and city test results in ELA.]

In first grade, the new phonics curriculum, Month by Month Phonics, is addressing this concern, but the teachers in the first grade have also expressed a need for more instructional time to be devoted to instruction in specific skills, such as inference making, drawing conclusions, determining main ideas, and utilizing contextual clues. Utilizing best practices in differentiated instruction should enable the needs of the future first grades to be met.

To address the need for improving writing skills, we will continue the staff development in preparing teachers in grades kindergarten through 2 with skills necessary to help students achieve proficiency on the fourth-grade ELA. Through professional development, teachers will receive strategies to address spelling and editing during the writing block. Children will also be exposed to instructional activities that encourage listening skills. This can be further achieved through the modeling of lessons and looking at exemplary student work.

The AUSSIE will continue modeling and providing staff development in kindergarten and grades 1 and 2, with an emphasis on grade 2. We will have at least one reading recovery teacher, if not two, on grade 1.

The student population is ever increasing in PS 22's ELL and special education categories. The needs of these pupils will be addressed through articulation sessions with the classroom and push-in/pull-out teachers. Best practices in differentiated instruction will be further modeled to assist teachers with these pupils.

In grade 2, we will continue to utilize different forms of assessment to drive instruction in the areas of reading comprehension, writing, and content area skills. The Diagnostic Reading Assessment has been ordered for all grades to drive this effort.

Teachers will administer a standardized test in May in grade 2 so that a longitudinal study can be conducted in grades 2 through 5 in literacy.

Teachers hope to address the development of writing skills by continuing staff development with their colleagues in the upper grades. Students should be exposed to instructional activities that encourage their listening skills. Second-grade instruction will build further on first-grade literacy activities and will further prepare the students for eventual proficiency on the fourth-grade ELA.

It is hoped that the literacy coach will continue to assist in the implementation of all the instructional concerns of the grade.

These strategies are expected to raise performance levels in the categories of our black, Hispanic, ELL, and special education populations.

Implications for the Instructional Program

- We will implement Everyday Math in grade 3 in a 75-minute math block.
- We will continue to provide children in need with very specific skill development in small-group settings. The push-in mode, whereby service providers worked hand in hand with classroom teachers, proved to be even more effective in mathematics instruction.
- We will continue to use Everyday Counts and other hands-on math manipulatives that make learning concrete operations and mathematical concepts fun. Children demonstrated high engagement in the lessons that were observed.
- We will continue professional development and sharing of best practices by staff members and regional staff assigned to our school.
- We will continue to use test sophistication materials to enable children to become familiar and at ease with timed test conditions.
- In order to have more comprehensive assessments, we will use Everyday Math periodic assessments, teacher observations, and portfolio assessments as well as the Princeton Review interim assessments to drive instruction. These will assist with the formation of AIS groups for intervention.
- There is continued need for weekend and extended-day intervention programs, provided this year with Federal Emergency Management Agency monies.
- We will continue to provide intensive Academic Intervention Services to all students who are not meeting standards.
- There will be intensive professional development in the use of specialized instructional strategies to meet the needs of special education.

Targeted populations of our pupils (ELL/LEP, black, Hispanic, special education) will receive additional services that will enable them to meet the New York State and City standards in mathematics. This will be accomplished using push-in/team-teaching strategies with ELL personnel and classroom teachers. We will schedule math cluster periods with self-contained special education classes. After-school tutoring in mathematics will provide services to targeted populations at PS 22. Articulation conferences will be scheduled with ELL personnel, classroom teachers, the math cluster teacher, and the school math coach. More computer software will be ordered for differentiated instruction in mathematics. The library will provide literature materials that will align with the math curriculum.

Data Analysis/Findings — Grade 4 Mathematics

There was an increase of 7.7% of fourth graders scoring level 3 or 4 on the New York State math test in 2003 as compared to 2002.

There was an increase of 3.2% of the students scoring level 1 on the New York State math test in 2003 as compared to 2002.

There was a decline in the scores of the special education students in 2003.

Results for ELL indicate a 7.2% increase in levels 3 and 4 and a 4.2% decrease in level 1.

Subgroup performance demonstrated that our special education and ELL populations did not perform as well on the 2003 New York State Exam. The gap in achievement will drive these strategies to raise the percentage of pupils who meet standards on the New York State Math Exam for our ELL and special education populations. These strategies implemented will improve performance levels.

Implications for the Instructional Program

- We will implement the Everyday Math program in grade 4 in September 2004 in a 75-minute math block.
- We will continue to provide children with very specific skill development in a small-group setting. The push-in model, whereby service providers work hand in hand with classroom teachers, proved to be even more effective in mathematics instruction.
- We will continue to use Everyday Counts and other hands-on math manipulatives that make learning concrete operations and mathematical concepts fun. Children demonstrated high engagement in lessons that were observed.
- We will continue professional development of best practices by staff members and regional staff assigned to our school.
- We will continue to use test sophistication materials to enable children to become familiar and at ease with timed test conditions.
- In order to have more comprehensive assessments, we will use Everyday Math periodic assessments, teacher observations, and portfolio assessments as well as the use of the Princeton Review to drive instruction. These will assist with the formation of AIS groups for intervention.

The needs of our ELL and special education student populations are further addressed through articulation sessions with classroom and push-in/pull-out teachers.

Part IV—Section A.1: Analysis of Student Achievement

2. English Language Arts

Data Analysis/Findings—ELA: State and City Test Results

There was a 0.2% increase in the percentage of students scoring a level 3 or 4 in 2003 as compared to 2002.

There was a 0.5% increases in the percentage of students scoring a level 1 in 2003.

Special education students showed an 8.2% decrease in scores of level 3 and 4 and an 8% increase in scores of level 1.

Results for ELL students showed a 4.4% increase in students scoring level 1 and a 12.7% decrease in students scoring a level 3 or 4. Overall, in grades 3, 4, and 5, the need exists to see growth from level 2 to levels 3 and 4 for our ELL students. Currently, 60% of the five children tested scored at level 1, as compared to 13.2% of our 604 English-proficient children.

In special education in 2003, 38 children were tested, and 47.5% of those tested scored in level 1. There is a need for these children to meet their IEP goals.

Because it is the first year of the New York State English as a Second Language Achievement Test (NYSESLAT), we have no statistics to compare their achievement levels with.

Implications for the Instructional Program

The student population is ever increasing in PS 22 ELL and special education populations. The needs of these pupils will be addressed and supported through weekly professional development and articulation sessions with classroom teachers, support staff, and push-in/pull-out teachers, as well as literacy and math coaches during the common preps. This will help develop best practices in differentiated instruction as well as workshop model strategies.

The ELL and special education teachers will also have access to technology available in the library during the literacy block upon request.

In all grades, the following will take place:

- Continued implementation of the 90-minute literacy block and daily writing activities
- Intensive Academic Intervention Services to all students who are not meeting city or state standards

- Leveled classroom libraries to be established in each classroom
- Professional development in the use of specialized instructional strategies to meet the needs of special populations

All teachers will further develop skills in the use of reading strategies that draw on scientifically based research in the dimensions of reading: (a) understanding how phonemes are connected to print—phonemic awareness, (b) being able to decode unfamiliar words, (c) being able to read fluently, (d) attaining background knowledge and vocabulary to foster reading comprehension, and (e) developing and maintaining motivation to read. In conjunction with teacher support, professional development will be provided to enhance the balanced literacy block to provide Internet access.

We will provide instruction to ELL students that will increase their English proficiency levels. The ESL teacher will align instruction with state and city standards to provide a push-in/pull-out program. The teacher will collaborate with each classroom teacher using a balanced literacy approach and leveled libraries. Outreach for parents will be provided through the parent coordinator, family associate, and PTA. Teachers will integrate vocabulary, concepts, and language functions in the content area in all lessons.

[*Note:* The next page, not excerpted, includes a summary of statistics and city test results in special education and mathematics.]

Part IV—Section A.1: Analysis of Student Achievement

3. Mathematics

Data Analysis/Findings—Grade 3 Math

The 2003 mathematics test shows an increase of 2.3% in third graders scoring a level 3 or 4 as compared to 2002.

There was a 6.4% reduction in the number of students scoring a level 1 in 2003 as compared to 2002. In special education, there was a 2.2% increase in students scoring levels 3 and 4 in 2003. More significantly, there was a 37.4% decrease in special education students scoring a level 1 in 2003; it can be presumed that a significant percentage of special education students moved from level 1 to level 2.

Subgroup performance demonstrated that targeted groups have not achieved the level of success that children in the white-race ethnicity category have on the New York City Exam in the level 3 category.

The gap in achievement will drive strategies to raise the percentage of pupils who meet standards on the New York City Math Exam.

- We will continue to provide intensive AIS to all students who are not meeting state standards.
- There will be intensive professional development in the use of specialized instructional strategies to meet the needs of special populations.
- The targeted population of ELL/LEP and special education students will receive additional services that will enable them to meet New York State and New York City standards in math, including the following:

    We will implement push-in/team-teaching strategies with the ELL teachers.

    ELL personnel and classroom teachers will meet regularly.

    Math cluster periods will be scheduled with self-contained special education classes.

    After-school tutoring in math will provide services to our targeted populations.

    Articulation conferences will be scheduled with ELL personnel, classroom teachers, math cluster teacher, and the school math coach.

    We will order computer software that will be geared toward differentiated instruction.

    The library cluster will provide literacy materials aligned to the math curriculum.

[*Note:* The data analysis and findings for grade 5 math are not excerpted. For brevity sake, I have excerpted only the analyses for early childhood, English, and math content areas, not for other academic areas that would usually be included.]

Part IV—Section B: Process for Reporting Needs Assessment Findings—Explain the process by which the findings of the needs assessment, as well as individual student and school data, were reported to school staff and parents. (Attach appropriate documentation.)

The school report card was distributed to each grade, and over the course of a month, personnel met to disaggregate the data. The grade meetings included support service personnel on the grade, namely, the Academic Intervention teacher, ELL teachers, resource room teachers, speech teachers, and counselors. The coaches also divided their time to meet with each grade in literacy and math. The assistant principal supervising kindergarten through grade 2 met with teachers to assist with data obtained from ECLAS and EPAL.

PS 22's Leadership Team reviewed the school report card in all areas. Committees were formed to address the areas in need of improvement. Those committees were advertised so that parents and teachers could volunteer schoolwide to participate in committees in developing the CEP and the findings of each grade. They discussed at length the variables contributing to the areas of concern.

Part IV—Section C: Identified Priorities for 2004–2005—Considering the findings and implications of your needs assessment, list your school's identified priorities for the 2004–2005 school year. These priorities will assist your school in the identification of goals and the development of objectives.

A review of the data indicates the following:

- The summary of grades 1 and 2 ECLAS results indicates a need to focus on phonemic awareness and comprehension skills.
- A review of the state and city test results in grades 3, 4, and 5 shows little growth in English language arts.
- Although our children are showing marked improvement in mathematics, more students need to move from level 1 to 2.

An analysis of the findings from a review of quantitative and qualitative data resulted in a determination of the following priorities:

- Improving student performance in literacy
- Improving student performance in math, with an emphasis on fifth grade
- Providing students with tools necessary to effectively utilize conflict resolution to improve discipline
- Improving home-school relationships in support of students' educational, social, and emotional needs

Part V: School Goals and Objectives

Directions: Identify the goals that have resulted from the needs assessment and develop objectives in the areas of English language arts (including ESL, where applicable), native language arts, mathematics, science, social studies (including civics and government, economics, history, and geography), foreign languages (for middle and high schools), technology, the arts, career/technical education, parent involvement, professional development, student support services, and other identified areas that will support the achievement of all students. (Be sure to address the needs of individual student subgroups.) School goals should reflect chancellor's initiatives and the superintendent's goals and should be prioritized based on an analysis of the data (Part IV). For each goal, state the objectives in specific, measurable, and observable terms (see guide), and provide a description of the proposed program. For each identified objective, complete an "Action Plan" using the format in Part VI.

Part V—Section A: English Language Arts (Including English as a Second Language, where applicable)

Goal: To increase student achievement in literacy for all students through standards-based data and data-driven instruction.

Objectives:

A.1. To achieve a 5% decrease for all students in grades 4–5 who scored a level 1 on the New York City and New York State ELA test.

A.2. To achieve a 5% decrease for at-risk students who scored levels 1 and 2 in grades K–3.

A.3. To achieve an increase of 5% in the number of students in grades 3–5 performing above level 2.

A.4. To achieve a 10% increase in the number of students in grade 1 meeting proficiency benchmarks as determined by and teacher assessment.

A.5. By June 2005, 55% of the mainstreamed ELLs will show an increase of at least one level of proficiency of the ELL program as measured by the NYSESLAT. Additionally, 20% of the resource/special education students will show an increase of at least one level of proficiency utilizing the same assessment tool.

Description of Proposed Instructional Strategies for English Language Arts (drawn from scientifically based research):

1. To implement the principles of learning in literacy-based environment.
2. To have the instructional team collaborate a plan with the AUSSIE, a reading recovery teacher, for professional development.
3. To use the Diagnostic Reading Assessment in all grades.

Part V—Section B: Native Language Arts (for schools with bilingual programs)

Goal: N/A

Objectives:

Part V—Section J: Parent Involvement

Goal: To strengthen the home/school connection to improve student performance.

Objectives: J.1. By June 2005, there will be an increase in parental involvement to support student outcomes in all subgroups.

Description of Proposed Parent Involvement Program: (Note: Title I schools must attach a copy of the Title I School Parent Involvement Policy and a sample of the School-Parent Compact.)

- PTA meetings where Student of the Month certificates are awarded
- Workshops in the family center
- Diversity of committees emanating from the School Leadership Team
- Literacy and Math Family Night
- Parent Coordinator and Family Associate outreach to the area civic associations

Part V—Section K: Professional Development

Goal: To implement an effective professional development program that is tiered to allow each staff member opportunities to address his or her specific needs in order to improve overall instruction.

Objectives:

K.1. Using data, principals will collaborate with stakeholders to sustain a dialogue on standards-based instruction that results in a sequential plan that targets student achievement and improved teaching performance.

K.2. Develop capacity of coaches to strengthen teaching and learning throughout the curriculum areas.

K. 3. Develop capacity of teachers to be risk takers and to implement best practices and strategies that work to improve achievement of all students.

K.4. Create professional study groups to allow discussions among staff regarding research, trends, and best practices in order to improve instruction.

K.5. Increase overall student performance by 10% using the Diagnostic Reading System in all classrooms.

Description of Proposed Professional Development Program:

The proposed professional development program at PS 22 will be tailored to offer a comprehensive tiered training program. Because of the varying levels of our staff's teaching experience, we believe it is important to structure our professional development based on staffing needs. These training opportunities will allow staff to have a menu of choices focused around Balanced Literacy, Everyday Math, and New Initiatives in order to improve instruction. This will allow staff to create a portfolio of professional development that complements all facets of the teachers' needs. Allowing staff to have input in their professional development will assist schoolwide initiatives in promoting a training model that complements staff strengths and improves teaching skills, thereby improving the quality of instruction and creating master teachers.

Part V—Section M: Other Identified Areas: Community Relations and Outside Agencies

Goal: To provide quality after-school care in a project-based learning environment.

Objectives: M.1. To improve instruction by providing instruction with a model that supports balanced literacy and increases school attendance by 5%.

Description of Proposed Strategy or Program:

- Hold monthly meetings with the PTA Executive Board to address PTA newsletters and meetings.
- Have the Family Associate continue outreach and follow-up with parents.
- Seek outside agencies for additional support: Staten Island Mental Health, Virtual Y, Latino Civic Association/Puerto Rican Institute, affiliation with Madison Square Garden.
- Continue school workshops in parenting skills at lunchtime.
- Continue to have reading volunteers from Staten Island Mental Heath.
- Create and maintain a community bulletin board to keep parents aware.
- Encourage service on Leadership Team and subcommittees through posting activities on the leadership bulletin board.
- Attend meetings for TASC best practices and partnership with Madison Square Garden.

Part VI: Action Plan—Goal A. English Language Arts

Directions: The Action Plan is a working document that clearly and briefly describes the objective(s) and activities to be undertaken for each particular goal. Actions should include a focus on the implementation of high-quality curriculum and instruction aligned with City and

State standards for *all* students (including general education; ELL/LEP students; students with disabilities; economically disadvantaged students; and students from major ethnic and racial groups, including white, black, Hispanic, Asian or Pacific Islander, and American Indian/ Alaskan Native), student support services, Academic Intervention Services that minimize removing children from the regular classroom (including the provision of extended learning time, i.e., extended school year, before- and after-school and summer programs, etc.), professional development, and parent involvement activities.

Goal: To increase student achievement in literacy for all students through standards-based data and data-driven instruction.

WHAT – Objective A.1	To achieve a 5% decrease in the number of students in grades 4–5 who scored a level 1 on the New York City (NYC) and New York State (NYS) ELA exam
WHO – Target population	Identified students in grades 4 and 5 who are at risk Identified subgroups as per school report card
HOW – Major tasks/activities	To provide supplemental services for at-risk students Literacy team and coach, teachers: classroom, ELL, AIS and Resource Room Heterogeneous grouping for cooperative learning groups, differentiated instruction Increase leveled libraries in every classroom
WHEN – Beginning date, frequency, and duration	September 2004 8:20 a.m.–2:50 p.m., except Tuesday for the extended day September through June
SUPPORT – Resources/cost/funding source	One push-in Pupils with Compensatory Educational Needs (PCEN) teacher in grade 4 @ $81,390 One push-in F-Status 0.2 teacher in PCEN One push-in AIS reading/math teacher @ $81,390: Title I After-school academics for at-risk children: $15,000 for personnel: Title I; $13,578 for materials to support program: PCEN

INDICATORS OF SUCCESS
– Interval of periodic review
– Instrument(s)/projected gains

Evidence of growth on assessments—
Princeton Review, teacher
evaluations, running records,
portfolios, NYC/NYS standardized
tests, ongoing review
and evaluation

ACCOUNTABILITY
– Person(s) or positions(s)
responsible

Principal, students, assistant
principals, parents, literacy
coach, teachers

[*Note:* The last section, excerpted below, includes detailed budget reports.]

CEP Action Plan—Budget Details

CEP Objective A.1_____   School: PS 22_____

List below budget items to be charged to each funding source to implement this goal. Use only one worksheet per funding source. The budget worksheet must be aligned with the action plan described in the CEP.

[*Note:* Many of the acronyms in this worksheet are specific to the school system for which the plan was written and thus are not spelled out.]

Title I	**SIG**	**Other**
PCEN	**State Magnet**	
Other:_____		
PCEN/LEP	**State Standards**	
Other:_____		
Part 154 LEP	**Title 2 Fed EGCR**	
Other:_____		
Title III LEP	**Other:**	
Other:_____		

(Continued)

Personnel Services:

Annualized and F-Status Positions

Name and EIS ID/ File Number Rate Cost	Position Title	FTE/PCT
TBD $81,390 = $81,390	One AIS teacher/push in	1 @
$0 = $0		@
$0 = $0		@
$0 = $0		@
$0 = $0		@
$0 = $0		@

Per Session/Per Diem Positions

Position/Subject Description Rate Cost	Position Title	FTE/PCT
After-school tutorial at risk $36.50 = $14,965	Teacher per session and	410 @
$0 = $0	Supervisor per session	@
$0 = $0		@
$0 = $0		@
$0 = $0		@

Total Personnel Cost: $96,355

Other Than Personnel Services:

Category/Title	Describe Items to Be Purchased	Amount
Instructional materials	See attached	@
$15,410		
To support program		@
$0		
		@
$0		
		@
$0		
		@
$0		

Total Other Than Personnel Services Cost: $15,410

TOTAL BUDGETED FROM THIS FUNDING SOURCE FOR THIS GOAL: $111,765

LIS Approval: _____

SGO Approval: _____

Reflective Questions

1. Do you really believe strategic initiatives are essential to your work as principal? How so? Be specific.

2. How much time would you devote to such strategic efforts? With all that you do, how would you find the time to strategically plan and conduct all the necessary follow-up activities involved in the process?

3. How would you go about initiating a strategic plan initiative?

4. What does strategic leadership mean to you, and why is it so important (if it is)? Explain.

5. What are specific ways you solicit school and community collaboration for your strategic initiatives?

6. What strategic practices or plans have you seen that really work well? Share with a colleague.

7. Which of the explanations above make the most sense to you?

8. Which of the explanations above make the least sense to you? Explain why.

9. After examining the sample Strategic Plan excerpts, identify the elements most useful to your work. Is the layout of the plan effective? Realize, of course, that the plan is partial and represents only one way of presenting information; other ways are feasible.

10. Can you think of principals who serve as exemplars in strategic leadership? What qualities do they possess? Are such qualities replicable? What could you learn from them?

11. How might you use action research in data-driven decision making? Provide a concrete example.

12. How are support for social justice issues and transformational change related to a principal's role as strategic leader?

13. What else would you need to know in developing a strategic plan?

See Resource B for a more detailed survey to assess your role as a strategic leader.

CHAPTER ONE

Introduction

"Whole-system change . . . requires educators to make sure their school districts create and maintain strategic alignment . . . to ensure that all the horses are pulling the wagon in the same direction."

—Francis M. Duffy

According to B. Davies and B. J. Davies (2005), "Strategic leadership is a critical component in the effective development of schools" (p. 10). They see strategic leadership not as a separate type of leadership (e.g., transformational leadership) but as a broader initiative that may span other leadership models (e.g., collaborative, instructional). In other words, strategic leadership skills are useful when principals aim to improve instructional programs, collaborate with broad constituencies, and transform their schools into (for instance) learning communities. The knowledge and skills of strategic leadership are critical to help accomplish these initiatives. In general, strategic leaders are committed to improving their organizations on many levels. Principals who exhibit strategic leadership believe and engage in the following activities, among others:

- Coordinating all functions and practices in the school so that everything works in harmony toward a common end
- Ensuring that all individuals share common goals

1

- Assessing the ability of the organization to respond to social, political, or interpersonal crises
- Adjusting the organization's mission to meet newly developing exigencies
- Imagining varied possibilities for the future

Serving as a strategic leader means that you are:

- Cognizant of pressures that may come to bear on the school organization
- Willing to respond promptly and with long-term planning initiatives
- Considerate of organizational resources
- Aware of strengths and weaknesses of individuals
- Ready to prioritize many requests for programs and resources
- Aware that strategic planning is not a linear, neat process but involves constant revision
- Interested in setting goals and articulating concrete plans to achieve them
- Disciplined and organized
- Never satisfied with success
- Committed to ongoing, whole-school improvement

As strategic leader of the school, you are continually, above all else, involved in strategic thinking. Strategic thinking "is predicated on involvement" of key participants. "To think strategically, . . . [principals] must be active, involved, connected, committed, alert, stimulated." It is "the calculated chaos" of your work that drives your "thinking, enabling you to build reflection on action as an interactive process. . . . Such thinking must not only be informed by the moving details of action, but be driven by the very presence of that action" (Mintzberg, 1994, p. 291).

According to Liedtka (1998), the following are the major attributes of strategic thinking.

A systems or holistic view. Strategic thinking is built on the foundation of a systems perspective. A strategic thinker has a mental model of the complete end-to-end system of value creation . . . and an understanding of the interdependencies it contains. . . . [The strategic thinker] sees [a] job not as a sum of its specific tasks, but as a contribution to a larger system that produces outcomes of value. . . .

A focus on intent. Strategic thinking is intent-driven. . . . Strategic intent provides the focus that allows individuals within an organization to . . . leverage their energy, to focus attention, to resist distraction, and to concentrate for as long as it takes to achieve a goal.

Thinking in time. Strategic thinkers link past, present, and future. . . . The gap between today's reality and intent for the future . . . is critical.

Hypothesis-driven. Strategic thinking . . . deals with hypothesis generating and testing as central activities . . . and avoids the analytic-intuitive dichotomy; . . . it is both creative and critical in nature. . . . This sequence [of hypothesis generating and testing] allows us to pose ever-improving hypotheses without forfeiting the ability to explore new ideas.

Intelligently opportunistic. The dilemma involved in using a well-articulated strategy to channel organizational efforts effectively and efficiently must always be balanced against the risks of losing sight of alternative strategies better suited to a changing environment. . . . There must be room for intelligent opportunism that not only furthers intended strategy but that also leaves open the possibility of new strategies emerging.

Further, pragmatic strategic leaders, according to Jones (2005), have a "realistic appraisal of the environment in which the school finds itself, the resources at its disposal and the opportunities that exist" (p. 6). They realize that, to be effective, strategic leadership must involve many others in the process. According to the Alliance for Nonprofit Management (2003–2004b):

An inclusive process:
- helps build both internal and external enthusiasm and commitment to the organization and its strategies. Individuals take on ownership of the goals and efforts to achieve the stated outcomes
- ensures that your informational data base reflects the needs and perceptions of internal individuals and external constituents
- incorporates a level of objectivity into the process. "Outsiders" can identify jargon or ask critical questions around which "insiders" might make assumptions
- develops foundations for future working relationships

- develops uniformity of purpose among all stakeholders
- establishes a continual information exchange among staff, management, customers, and other key stakeholders

This book represents one aspect of a principal's work. Each book in the series addresses a specific, important role or function of a principal. Discussing each separately, however, is quite artificial and a bit contrived. In fact, all seven forms of leadership (instructional, cultural, ethical/spiritual, collaborative, operational, school-community, and strategic) form an undifferentiated whole. Still, we can glean much from a more in-depth analysis into each form of leadership. It is with such understanding that this book is framed. Strategic leadership reflects an educational paradigm based on the following assumptions or premises:

- Organizational life is dynamic, complex, chaotic, and unpredictable, yet strategic leaders examine internal and external data to discern any predictable patterns or trends that will help in initiating a strategic vision or plan.
- Strategic planning helps a school establish direction and goals for the future by asking how the school may be different 5, 7, even 10 years from now.
- Strategic planning is an ever-changing, flexible, and creative process that requires leaders to exhibit patience and tolerance for ambiguity.
- Strategic leadership thrives in a learning community wherein educators demonstrate their long-term commitments to curricular and instructional excellence.
- You, as principal, play the most vital role in strategic planning as initiator, facilitator, motivator, assessor, and transformer.
- Strategic leaders are committed to participatory school management and leadership.
- Strategic planning is supported by a systematic assessment program aimed to collect data to inform decision making to improve educational programming.
- Strategic leaders are visionary iconoclasts who take calculated risks for the benefit of the school organization.
- Strategic leaders are astute politicians able to utilize organizational resources to accomplish their goals.
- Not content with the status quo, strategic leaders aim to transform the school organization to higher levels of performance and overall success.

> ### Reflective Questions
>
> 1. Consider leaders you have known. Assess their strategic leadership skills. What stands out as particularly noteworthy? Unworthy?
>
> 2. Assess the degree to which strategic planning exists in your school. What have been your experiences with strategic leadership?
>
> 3. What strategic leadership challenges do you face? Explain.
>
> 4. React to the assumptions or premises listed above. Which make the most sense to you?
>
> 5. What is the benefit of a strategic plan? Describe a school in which such a plan exists.

* * * * * * * * * * * * * * * *

This book and series are also aligned with standards established by the prominent Educational Leadership Constituent Council (ELCC). ELCC standards are commonly accepted by most educational organizations concerned with preparing high-quality educational leaders and as such are most authoritative (Wilmore, 2002). The ELCC, an arm of the National Council for the Accreditation of Teacher Education, developed six leadership standards used widely in principal preparation. These standards formed the basis for this book and series:

1.0: Candidates who complete the program are educational leaders who have the knowledge and ability to promote the success of all students by facilitating the development, articulation, implementation, and stewardship of a school or district vision of learning supported by the school community.

2.0: Candidates who complete the program are educational leaders who have the knowledge and ability to promote the success of all students by promoting a positive school culture, providing an effective instructional program, applying best practices to student learning, and designing comprehensive professional growth plans for staff.

3.0: Candidates who complete the program are educational leaders who have the knowledge and ability to promote the success of all students by managing the organization, operations, and resources in a way that promotes a safe, efficient, and effective learning environment.

4.0: Candidates who complete the program are educational leaders who have the knowledge and ability to promote the success of all students by collaborating with families and other community members, responding to diverse community interests and needs, and mobilizing community resources.

5.0: Candidates who complete the program are educational leaders who have the knowledge and ability to promote the success of all students by acting with integrity, fairly, and in an ethical manner.

*6.0: Candidates who complete the program are educational leaders who have the knowledge and ability to promote the success of all students by understanding, responding to, and influencing the larger political, social, economic, legal, and cultural context.

* This standard is addressed in this book.

Readers should also familiarize themselves with standards from the Interstate School Leaders Licensure Consortium and the National Association of Elementary School Principals (NAESP) (see, e.g., http://www.ccsso.org/projects/Interstate_School_Leaders_Licensure_Consortium/ and http://www.boyercenter.org/basicschool/naesp.shtml).

Another important point to make in this Introduction is for you to realize that you may think that strategic leadership may not have immediate payback, as some other forms of leadership do. However, underestimating the long-range impact of strategic leadership is short-sighted. Taking the time to frame a long-range vision supported by meaningful goals and objectives is vital to your school's success. Strategic leadership and planning will result, in the long term, in high student achievement for all students in your school.

* * * * * * * * * * * * * * *

In order to establish a framework for the three chapters, Figure 1.1 illustrates the role of the principal attempting to facilitate and influence the critical elements of strategic leadership (i.e., planning strategically, encouraging data-driven decision making, and mediating the political environment, corresponding to Chapters 2, 3, and 4, respectively). Effective principals strive to transform their schools into cutting-edge institutions that understand the nature of change, promote a sense of social justice, and build leadership capacity and sustainability. When

Figure 1.1   A Strategic Leadership Model That Promotes Student
                Achievement

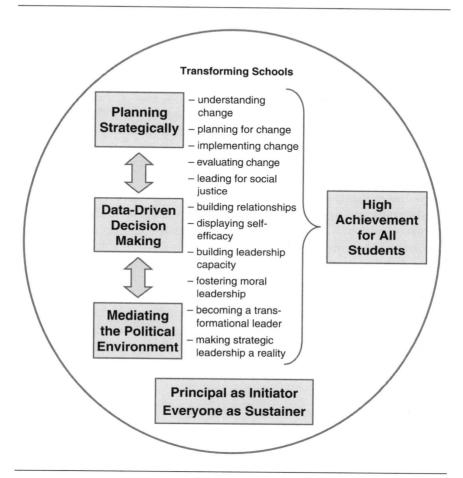

these aspects of strategic leadership work at their best, a culture of student achievement for all students is established and maintained.

Allow me to offer a word on chapter format and presentation of information. Information in each of the three chapters is presented as concisely as possible to make for easy and quick reference reading. Each chapter begins with boxed material called "What You Should Know About." The box will list and briefly explain the concepts covered in each chapter. Certainly, as mentioned earlier, each chapter will not cover every bit of information there is to know about a given topic. Each chapter culls, though, essential knowledge, skills, and dispositions necessary for a successful principal.

A brief word on chapter organization is in order to facilitate reading. The first chapter includes some best practices for initiating and sustaining a strategic planning initiative. After reviewing some practical strategies for doing so, the second chapter highlights practices for collecting data for the purpose of making critical instructional and curricular decisions to enhance various goals in the strategic plan. The final chapter focuses on the knowledge and skills of transformative leadership that are so much part of a strategic leader. Taken together, these three chapters provide you with information and strategies that can set you on a course of strategizing for the future of your organization. This book, however, is not meant to be the definitive treatise on strategic leadership; rather, my goal is to raise some relevant issues for your consideration. It is my hope that the ideas in this book will give you pause to think about your own role in strategic leadership.

As a concluding activity to this Introduction, read the boxed material below, which contains 10 quotations meant to inspire and, more important, to provoke critical thinking about your role as strategic leader. Read each quotation, and ask yourself these questions:

- What does the author convey about strategic leadership?
- Critique the quotation. Does the thought reflect your beliefs? Explain.
- What practical step(s) could you take to actualize the idea behind each quotation?

Some Key Quotations Related to Strategic Leadership

"If we want change to matter, to spread, and to last, then the system in which leaders do their work, must make sustainability a priority."

—Andy Hargreaves and Dean Fink

"A successful strategic planning process will examine and make informed projections about environmental realities to help an organization anticipate and respond to change by clarifying its mission and goals; targeting spending; and reshaping its programs."

—Richard Mittenthal

"The challenges are abundant, the responsibility awesome, and the need for moral leadership incalculable."

—Carolyn M. Shields

"Leading change in public education is tumultuous work. It is relentlessly intense, enormously complex, and often downright chaotic."

—Scott Thompson

"For strategic decision making to be effective, constraints and obstacles, as well as opportunities and challenges that impact the decision choice, must be identified."

—Petra E. Snowden and Richard A. Gorton

"I believe courageous, passionate, and visionary leaders . . . need to recognize that their effectiveness as change-leaders is the result of the skillful interplay of power, politics, and ethics."

—Francis M. Duffy

"Principals and other school leaders have been given a different charge: take an abundance of student data, mostly in the form of assessments, and turn this data into information to be used in improving educational practice."

—Jeffrey C. Wayman, Steve Midgley, and Sam Stringfield

"Strategic leaders are able to picture a range of possibilities several stages ahead of the current phase of organizational development."

—Jeff Jones

"Leading schools through complex reform agendas requires new leadership that goes far beyond improving test scores."

—Michael Fullan

"The principal's job is to design and nurture an environment in which teachers can more readily take charge of their work."

—Robert J. Starratt

CASE STUDY AND REFLECTIVE QUESTIONS

Strategic planning may come in various forms. Ms. Vincenza Gallassio is in her second year as principal in an urban elementary school in New York

Note: Many thanks to Ms. Vincenza Gallassio, who has allowed me to use her Principal Performance Review and her personal strategic plan as an example of how one principal strives for strategic leadership. Thanks also to E. Scott Miller, who serves as Ms. Gallassio's supervisor and evaluator. Their strong professional relationship represents, in this author's view, best practice for principal professional development as well as strategic planning.

City. Mr. E. Scott Miller, a local instructional superintendent charged with mentoring and evaluating Ms. Gallassio, is a strong supporter. "Ms. Gallassio is a forward thinker. Well organized and thoughtful, she understands the key ingredients of effective school leadership. She's a planner, but with sense and creativity. She thinks out of the box and knows how to generate enthusiasm, even among the more experienced teachers. Her keen sense of vision and energy make her one of the region's up and coming stars." He wrote her the following letter at the end of the first month of the school year.

September 29, 2004
Ms. Vincenza Gallassio
Principal (IA)
Public School XX

Re: <u>Principal Performance Review, September 2004</u>

Dear Ms. Gallassio:

Your leadership is essential to the effectiveness of the instructional program in your school. Governance legislation requires the Superintendent to evaluate the performance of each principal with respect to educational effectiveness and school performance, including effectiveness of promoting student achievement and parental involvement and maintaining school discipline. The Principal Review process is designed for you to set your goals and objectives for the school year in consultation with the Superintendent to ensure that the priority needs of your school will be addressed. We will meet in October to develop your goals and objectives for the 2004–2005 school year in the areas of:

- Instructional leadership
- Organizational leadership
- Staff development
- Student support services
- Community relations and communication

Your goals and objectives must support your school's Comprehensive Educational Plan (CEP)—include specific activities and a timeline. In addition to your written summary of your goals and objectives in the five areas listed above, please bring written responses and be prepared to discuss the following:

- What trends are indicated by your historical and your disaggregated test data?
- What are the major goals of your CEP?
- How do you organize your school, your office, and your day to support and enhance student achievement?
- What are the three instructional "bottom line" components that must be visible in every classroom?
- How will you communicate your bottom lines to your staff?
- What is the focus for your own professional development and that of your assistant principals and your staff?
- How will you organize the 18 sessions of 100 minutes of professional development time, faculty conferences, grade and/or subject conferences to ensure consistent progress toward your goals and performance targets?
- Who are the members of your instructional improvement team?
- How will you work with your coaches to ensure consistent progress toward your goals?
- What is working? What is not working?
- What are your strengths? Your weaknesses?
- Who are your strong teachers? How will you use them as a lever for change?
- Who are your weak teachers? How will you assist them?
- Who are your new teachers? How will you support them?
- Who are your at-risk students? Is there an academic intervention plan in place?
- How will you support the English-language learner (ELL) and children with special needs in all classrooms?
- How will your staff consistently assess and document student progress toward meeting the standards?
- What is your plan to monitor teacher planning and preparation?
- How will classroom libraries be integrated into the daily instructional program?
- What is your plan to increase student achievement in literacy and mathematics?
- How will you work with your parent engagement officer to increase parent involvement and improve the home-to-school connection?

I look forward to meeting with you in October to complete Step I of your 2004–2005 Principal Performance Review (PPR).

Sincerely,

E. Scott Miller

E. Scott Miller
Local Instructional Superintendent
Region 7–Cohort 3

Prompted by the review and Ms. Gallassio's strong belief in strategic leadership, she articulated the following plan in response to Mr. Miller's request and with his guidance:
Three Bottom Lines

✓ **Change of culture and climate of school building**
  o Professional development to meet the needs of staff
  o Create conditions that support transformational change
  o Through modeling of lessons, inter/intravisitations of lessons and actively supervising classroom walk-throughs
  o Stability of instruction across grade levels
  o Focused communication of goals and changes to assistant principals and coaches

✓ **Classroom libraries as an integral part of instruction**
  o Implement physical changes in classrooms
    • Leveled libraries
    • Centers
    • Clustering of desks
    • Rugged area for instruction
  o Differentiation of instruction
  o Building capacity for teachers to assess students

✓ **Common planning leading to consistency of instruction**
  o Conception of extended collaboration time as nonnegotiable for team/support teaching
  o Implementation of minimally three common preps per grade-level team with the inclusion of special education, bilingual, and dual-language teachers
  o Teachers setting personal goals that will be supported by the coaching and administrative staff

Instructional Leadership
Goal: To increase achievement in literacy for all students through standards-based, data-driven instruction

✓ By June 2005, implementation of Reading First in Grades K–3 with fidelity to the program using the Five Dimensions of Reading as a basis for reading instruction during the uninterrupted Literacy Block as measured by standardized tests (e.g., ECLAS-2, Dynamic Indicators of Basic Early Literacy Skills [DIBELS], EPAL, and the Terranova).
  o Instructional team meetings every two weeks with regional support
  o Weekly professional development team meetings

✓ By June 2005, implementation of the Workshop Model in Grades 4–5 to put into practice the Balanced Literacy Workshop Model as prescribed by the Comprehensive Approach to Balanced Literacy as measured by standardized tests: both New York City (NYC) and New York State (NYS) exams.
  o Weekly professional development team meetings
  o Intervisitation of schools that support Balanced Literacy Model

✓ By June 2005, implementation of the Writer's Workshop in all classrooms will be visible in students' work and will be measured by the NYC and NYS standardized tests.
  o Standards grade-level writing conferences
  o In-depth focus of the characteristics of writing

✓ Writing standards

✓ Writing rubrics
  o Oral rehearsal of writings

✓ "Think alouds"

✓ Guided writing

Goal: To implement an instructional program that is aligned with NYC and NYS standards and that will improve student performance in mathematical skill, concepts, and problem solving in Grades K–5

✓ By June 2005, implementation of Everyday Math Workshop Model in Grades K–5 using the Workshop Model to drive

instruction that meets the needs of students as measured by the NYC and NYS standardized tests.
- o Weekly professional development team meetings
- o Continuation of lunch math team meetings

Organizational Leadership
Goal: To provide an environment where the staff and administration can acquire new knowledge and skills and implement them in our daily practice

- ✓ By June 2005, the objective is to facilitate professional development of assistant principals in an environment of managerial organization in which individuals undertake responsibilities delegated.
  - o Reading *Supervision That Improves Teaching* by S. Sullivan and J. Glanz
  - o Developing curriculum practices for implementation
  - o Delegating organizational responsibilities

- ✓ By June 2005, the objective is to delegate managerial duties to various personnel to work collaboratively with all stakeholders to create a learning community.
  - o Secretaries to be active participants
  - o Guidance counselors and assistant principals to create plans

Staff Development
Goal: To implement an effective program in professional development based on identified needs that results in improved performance of all students

- ✓ By June 2005, the objective is to construct a core team of members that will further the vision set forth to support adult learning in a nonthreatening environment through the sustaining of a professional development team.

- ✓ By June 2005, the objective is to build the capacity of building coaches and teacher leaders to drive the professional development that meets the needs of the adult learners.
  - o Professional development activities
  - o Team building

✓ By June 2005, the objective is to differentiate professional development to meet the needs of staff through assessments, observations, and other focused conversations.
  o Surveys
  o Assessments
  o Reflections

Student Support Services
Goal: To provide all students with access to services that promote student academic, social/emotional, and physical development

✓ Throughout the 2004–2005 academic year, the objective is to organize the creation and use of a database of "at-risk" students with biweekly meetings.
  o Intervention specialists to discuss intervention practices
  o Professional development to meet the needs of at-risk practitioners

✓ Throughout the 2004–2005 academic year, the objective is to have biweekly meetings with school assessment team to organize and facilitate the course of action for students with needs.
  o Discussion of open cases (201)

✓ Throughout the 2004–2005 academic year, the objective is to use data to drive instruction to meet the needs of students.
  o Use of ECLAS-2, DIBELS, and other standardized test results
  o Creation of assessment binder

Community Relations and Communication
Goal: To increase parent involvement and capacity in school initiatives to support outcomes for all students

✓ Throughout the 2004–2005 academic year, the objective is to reach out to community members, create relationships that motivate parental involvement, and begin relationships with local learning institutions.
  o Creation of school Web site
  o Parent newsletter
  o School leadership team
    • Title 1 Parent Involvement Team
    • Parent Advisory Committee

     o Wagner College
- Student teachers
- Student observers
- Participation in the creation of supervisory program with Dr. J. Glanz

     o College of Staten Island English as a Second Language (ESL) program
- Adult ESL program
- Student teachers

     o Outreach to local board of realtors

She now addressed some of the questions posed by Mr. Miller:

- What trends are indicated by your historical and your disaggregated test data?

The trends over the last three years show a steady decline in ELA in levels 3 and 4. In 2004, there was a small increase of 3.8% from the previous year. Disaggregating the data shows that the largest number of students historically scores at level 2. Further analysis shows that the number of students in this level is approximately the same when referred to as high, medium, or low. The ELL population scores approximately 7% points lower than the English-proficient students.

The math scores over the last three years have shown a steady small increase (35.3 in 2003 and 38.4 in 2004). The largest numbers of students are in level 2. Further analysis shows that the number of students in this level is approximately the same when referred to as high, medium, or low.

- What are the major goals of your CEP?

The major goals of the CEP are to implement the Reading First Initiative. The restructuring plan indicates that the needs of the ELL students are to be met through the initial implementation of the Dual Language program.

- How do you organize your school, your office, and your day to support and enhance student achievement?

The school day is organized with a daily morning cabinet meeting with the assistant principals. The teachers are informed through a daily "Items of the Day" posted above the time clock. Each supervisor is expected to minimally walk through the grades they supervise daily. At least three times a week, a team of two or more supervisors will have a focused walk through classrooms. These walk-throughs will lead to further instructional changes.

The delegation of school responsibilities will be completed by the administrative team. An end-of-day sharing of walk-throughs, concerns, and other matters will take place at the end of the day.

- What are the three instructional "bottom lines" that must be visible in every classroom?

    Leveled library

    Word wall

    Centers

- How will you communicate your bottom lines to your staff?

The bottom lines will be communicated through daily feedback to teachers, coaches, and administrative staff. The vision will be presented to the staff at all faculty conferences, United Federation of Teachers consultation committee meetings, and Instructional team meetings. The monthly schoolwide readings will promote the ideas that are to be communicated to students and faculty. For example, the September book of the month will deal with collaboration.

- What is the focus for your own professional development and that of your assistant principals and your staff?

The administrative team is reading the book *Supervision That Improves Teaching* by S. Sullivan and J. Glanz.

- How will you organize the 18 sessions of 100 minutes of professional development time, faculty conferences, grade and/or subject conferences to ensure consistent progress toward your goals and performance targets?

The professional development sessions will initially focus on shared reading and move into assessments and guided reading. The needs of the staff will be looked at as individuals and as a group. The faculty conferences will focus on broader topics and chancellor mandates. The grade-level conferences will alternate between teachers participating in model lessons, discussions from the Harcourt AUSSIE, and meetings with teachers' immediate supervisors.

- Who are the members of the instructional improvement team?

The members were chosen by the grade constituents, cluster representation, and out-of-classroom personnel, along with all coaches and administrators. The team will be enhanced by regional representatives.

- How will you work with coaches to ensure consistent progress toward your goals?

The coaches will be working during extended collaboration time with teachers on a consistent basis. Each coach is expected to work closely with one teacher for one period a day. The coaches will meet as a group on their own. The coaches will debrief and set concerns to administrative staff as they arise (e.g., ECLAS coverage, DIBELS testing).

- What is working? What is not working?
- What are your strengths? Your weaknesses?
- Who are your strong teachers? How will you use them as a lever for change?
- Who are your weak teachers? How will you assist them?
- Who are your new teachers? How will you support them?

Discussed at PPR in October.

- Who are your "at-risk" students? Is there an academic intervention plan in place?

A database of at-risk students has been created. The database contains the standardized scores, previous hold-overs, support services, and other relevant information. The academic intervention plan has been written and is in place.

- How will you support ELL students and children with special needs in all classrooms?

The Title 1 paraprofessionals and the academic intervention teachers will work with students in a push-in and pull-out model. Students identified in these two categories will be monitored and discussed with each group of teachers. The intervention liaison will debrief the teachers on her monthly meetings.

- How will your staff consistently assess and document student progress toward meeting the standards?

Beginning in January we will be creating an assessment binder. Teachers have been gathering information on students (both soft and hard data). These data will be organized for use to improve and focus instruction.

- How will classroom libraries be integrated into the daily instructional program?

The classroom libraries are one of the "bottom lines." Teachers have spent a great deal of time leveling and moving students into their use.

- What is your plan to increase student achievement in literacy and mathematics?

The plan is to move student achievement by changing teacher practice. The adult learning is the primary focus. Through staff development, modeled lessons, visitations of other schools, and support of teachers, this can be achieved.

- How will your work with your parent engagement officer to increase parent involvement and improve the home-to-school connection?

The parental involvement focus initially will come from the Parent Advisory Committee. The parents want to have a voice in how the Title 1 Parent Engagement money is to be spent. The meetings have been productive and have led to other initiatives. The Parent Center continues to be a focus in the school.

Reflective Questions

1. React to Ms. Gallassio's ambitious goals. Are they realistic, accomplishable? Explain.

2. React to her three "bottom lines." Are they areas you would highlight in your work as principal?

3. React to her goals and objectives. What resources, support mechanisms, and other things would she need to actualize them?

4. React to the way she answered Mr. Miller's questions. How do her responses reflect her overarching bottom lines and goals?

5. What advantages can you identify for such an approach to principal professional development and strategic planning?

6. What educational benefits are there for student learning when principals engage in such activities?

7. What other approaches to strategic planning could you take?

8. How might you demonstrate your commitment to strategic planning?

As mentioned in the Introduction, the chapter that follows builds upon the preceding information by highlighting some "best practices" for helping you engage in meaningful strategic planning initiatives so crucial for forward-looking leadership. These ideas are not meant to be exhaustive of the topic, but merely a means to encourage thinking related to strategizing for the success of all.

CHAPTER TWO

Best Practices in Planning Strategically

"No matter how well long-range and strategic plans are developed and implemented, there are usually things that come up that necessitate more resources than most schools actually have."

—Elaine L. Wilmore

"Among the final steps toward institutional transformation, leaders will want to consolidate the improvements made, track and report on successes to stakeholders, and continue to inspire still more change."

—Robert C. Dickeson

"Optimal performance rests on the existence of a powerful shared vision that evolves through wide participation. . . . The test of greatness of a dream is that it has the energy to lift people out of their moribund ways to a level of being and relating from which the future can be faced with more hope."

—Robert Greenleaf

Research confirms that school leaders must remain "strategically intelligent" in order to manage and sustain the educational reform so vital to an organization (see, e.g., B. Davies & B. J. Davies, 2005). Change is an undeniable reality for any organization. Not all change means a school will be better off or improve, but no improvement can occur without planned change. As a principal, if you want to improve your school, as you of course want to do, you must be well versed in strategic leadership.

According to Davies and Davies (2005), school leaders are involved in five "key activities":

- Direction setting
- Translating strategy into action
- Aligning the people and the organization to the strategy
- Determining effective intervention points
- Developing strategic capabilities

Strategic principals look to the future and base their vision on fundamental beliefs about various aspects of the school (e.g., curricular, instructional, interpersonal). These beliefs are shared and discussed widely with internal and external constituencies. This vision, or "moral purpose," as Davies and Davies (2005, p. 12) refer to it, translates into strategy development to actualize the vision. According to Davies and Davies, "The function of strategy is to translate the moral purpose and vision into reality" (p. 12). Having a sense of where a school is and where it needs to go is critical in the strategic process.

The second phase is translating this strategy into action. B. J. Davies (2002, cited in B. Davies & B. J. Davies, 2005) highlights a "four-stage ABCD approach of translating strategy into action":

- **Stage 1: Articulation**—This phase refers to communication about the strategies. As principal, you may initiate conversations, but more important, you encourage wide participation among key parties. Communication can occur also in more formal ways, that is, by writing down strategic goals and methods used to accomplish them. Finally, establishing the structure to facilitate articulation is critical. Structural support mechanisms may include scheduling common prep periods among faculty for planning, allowing for released time during the school day or a day away from the school to attend a conference, and so forth.

- **Stage 2: Building**—This phase doesn't necessarily follow the previous one but is really meant to rally faculty and staff around the strategy to gain their input and support. You can build support through use of logos, T-shirts, informal and formal meetings, and so on. Building refers to extending the vision and support for it.

- **Stage 3: Creating**—This phase emphasizes your discovering and utilizing creative ways to dialogue with others to motivate them to share a "conceptual or mental map of the future." Davies and Davies (2005) explain, "What strategic leaders are able to do is step back and articulate the main features of the current organization, which might be called the strategic architecture of the school" (p. 14). Scheduling a retreat of sorts might be one suggested creative forum to work on this stage.

- **Stage 4: Defining**—This phase involves identifying "desired outcomes" and designing specific strategies to achieve them.

In all efforts involving strategic leadership, aligning people's interests and abilities with ways of promoting strategic initiatives is critical to the entire process and represents a third phase or key activity of a strategic leader. Once you identify key people and the roles they can play and are willing to play, you must keep them motivated and on target. Davies and Davies (2005) discuss several ideas for doing so, including:

- *Strategic conversations*—involving ongoing, frequent, formal and informal dialogues with individuals and groups inside and outside the school
- *Strategic participation*—encouraging meaningful, not superficial, involvement every step of the way
- *Strategic motivation*—creating an atmosphere of trust and confidence in your leadership and, more important, in the larger strategic effort
- *Strategic capability*—bringing together diverse individuals who are willing to agree to disagree in an atmosphere of mutual respect

A fourth phase involves determining effective intervention points. Davies and Davies (2005) talk about "strategic timing" as crucial for overall success. When people are not ready, for instance, or institutional mechanisms that support strategic planning are not firmly in place, it is not an opportune time to initiate or move forward on goals of the strategic initiative. Davies and Davies explain, "Strategic timing affects all the people in the school community. If the strategic timing is wrong I can have devastating effects on the school. People will be divided, and realizing the strategy will therefore be impossible" (p. 17).

> *"Strategic leaders have a great sense of timing. . . . They and their schools are alert and ready to seize an opportunity."*
>
> —Jeff Jones

Developing strategic capabilities is the final key activity, according to Davies and Davies (2005). Building a learning community (Sullivan & Glanz, 2006) in which individuals are committed to a larger goal than themselves and are willing to share, collaborate, take risks, problem-solve, agree to disagree in an atmosphere of civility and mutual respect, and so forth is essential for strategic capability.

Although these activities or phases are important for successful strategic planning, no strategic initiative is complete or even possible without a leader: you. Davies and Davies (2005) identify four characteristics that successful strategic leaders display:

- "Strategic leaders have a dissatisfaction or restlessness with the present" (p. 20).
- "Strategic leaders prioritize their own strategic thinking and learning" (p. 20).
- "Strategic leaders create mental models to frame their own understanding and practice" (p. 21).
- "Strategic leaders have powerful personal and professional networks" (p. 22).

Strategic leaders are rarely, if ever, satisfied with the way things are, the status quo. They are imaginative and restless. They continually seek better ways of doing things. They enjoy planning for the future. These leaders constantly spend time in reflection about their goals and plans for their school. Realizing the complex nature of school life, they reach out to others to enhance their own understanding, because they realize that their own perspective might be limited. Finally, principal leaders who plan strategically build and sustain meaningful partnerships or networks of individuals who can advise them or support their ideas and initiatives. Davies and Davies (2005) underscore this point: "Strategic leaders place a high importance on networks and networking to draw in ideas and inspiration for strategic change and development" (p. 22).

Reflective Questions

1. What is your commitment to strategic leadership? Explain in depth.

2. In what specific areas or activities would you see your involvement as most critical? React to the "key activities" enumerated by Davies and Davies (2005) above.

3. To what degree do you display the four characteristics of strategic leaders mentioned above? Explain.

4. What are some specific strategies you would employ in planning strategically? Provide concrete examples.

5. What are the advantages and disadvantages of "busying" yourself in strategic leadership initiatives?

6. Consider leaders you have known and know, and describe how they approach strategic leadership. What do they do that stands out in your mind? Would you call them strategic leaders? Explain why or why not.

The boxed material below summarizes the ideas highlighted in this chapter. The list is not exhaustive, but is merely meant to highlight some key concepts and ideas that successful strategic leaders should understand as they go about planning. The "best practices" highlighted in the remainder of this chapter are those that the author has utilized in his practice as a school administrator, has used in working closely with other principals, or has culled from the research literature. Brief reflective activities follow each major concept to provoke thought on ways to implement or further understand each idea. Please note that strategic planning can be overwhelming for any principal. Models across the country vary. Some schools adopt a model that closely follows the accreditation process advocated by regional associations. Take the information that follows and apply it to your own situation.

What You Should Know About Planning Strategically

- **Nine Steps to Successful Planning**—We review Mittenthal's (2002) nine steps for successful strategic planning.
- **Promoting Vision, Mission, and Goals**—We highlight some practical suggestions from Ramsey (2003) on vision making.

- **Conducting a SWOT Analysis**—Famous SWOT analysis is explained, in part, with information from the Alliance for Nonprofit Management (2003–2004c).
- **A Guide to Strategic Planning**—Lyddon's (1999) 10 steps to strategic planning are detailed.
- **West Morris Regional High School District's** (2000–2005) **Long-Range Plan**—An example of a succinct plan is excerpted.

1. NINE STEPS TO SUCCESSFUL PLANNING

These steps are among the most succinct and useful that can be found in the literature (see Mittenthal, 2002).

Step 1: Possess a clear and comprehensive grasp of external opportunities and challenges.

As a strategic leader, you should frame your strategic vision in light of social, economic, and political realities and trends. As schools, for instance, move toward more inclusive practices, you might consider opportunities to implement collaborative team teaching classes. Visiting schools that already have such classes and learning from failures and successes of other principals is a good idea. Maintaining contact with local, state, and national networks as well as reading literature from national associations (e.g., National Association of Secondary School Principals [NASSP], NAESP) and attending conferences will keep you abreast of the latest trends and developments.

Step 2: Undertake a realistic and comprehensive assessment of the organization's strengths and weaknesses.

Every organization can identify its assets and areas that need more attention. Doing so is critical to your success as strategic leader (see discussion of SWOT below).

Step 3: Utilize an inclusive approach.

Include varied constituent groups in the planning process. Invite input on a regular basis. Listen and act on people's suggestions so that they really believe you care about their views. Collaborative leadership skills are necessary for strategic leaders (see volume on this topic in the Principal Leadership Series).

Step 4: Convene an empowered planning committee.

Participation, as mentioned, is critical. Form a committee of interested parties. Schedule in-school time for meetings, and empower the committee with decision-making authority.

Step 5: Involve senior leadership.

Keeping your superintendent or representative informed at each critical stage is recommended. Solicit senior leaders' advice and input. Ask them to inform you about the extent to which they want to remain involved.

Step 6: Learn from best practices.

Survey comparable schools in your locale or state for best practices. Every good educator "borrows" good ideas from elsewhere. Make sure you give credit, of course, and match the idea to the unique situation in your school.

Step 7: Establish clear priorities and an implementation plan.

Your committee can assist in this step. Of course, you should be aware of all developments at every stage. Share and articulate your vision and priorities. Achieve consensus whenever possible. At times, you will have to make difficult decisions about competing priorities. As long as you make known the criteria you have established to determine which priorities get funded and which ones do not, you'll be in a good position to minimize resentment and complaints. In reality, however, some people will never be satisfied. That's a political and interpersonal reality of our job.

Step 8: Have patience.

Ups and downs will naturally occur. Expect upsets, and expect the unexpected. Also, strategic development takes time, as you are balancing many complicated factors. Mittenthal (2002) provides some advice: "It is important to keep things on course and maintain momentum, but rushing is counter productive" (p. 8).

Step 9: Affirm a commitment to change.

Mittenthal (2002) states:

No matter how relevant its original mission, no organization can afford to shackle itself to the same goals, programs, and operating methods year after year. . . . strategies need to be revisited regularly. Sometimes all that's needed is fine-tuning; other times, a more fundamental rethinking of goals and opportunities may be required. If they are to remain viable and effective, organizations must be prepared to change as extensively as conditions require. (p. 9)

> *"The transformational leader is one who motivates followers to perform above expectations."*
>
> —Vernadine Thomas

Mittenthal (2002) concludes:

A strategic plan is not a wish list, a report card, or marketing tool. It is certainly not a magic bullet or a quick cure for everything that ails an organization. . . . What a strategic plan can do is shed light on an organization's unique strengths and relevant weaknesses, enabling it to pinpoint new opportunities or the causes of current or projected problems. (p. 9)

Reflective Questions

1. What do you think about the nine steps explained above? How might you utilize Mittenthal's ideas?

2. What is one practical strategy you can employ to put into practice each step above? Be specific as possible.

---

2. PROMOTING YOUR VISION, MISSION, AND GOALS

Strategic planning is predicated most fundamentally on an articulated, well-established, and accepted vision, mission, and series of goals for the school. Don't blur the difference between a vision and a mission. "Vision is knowing where you want to be or what you want to become. . . . Mission is your reason for being and the work you pursue to realize your vision" (Kaser, Mundry, Stiles, & Loucks-Horsley, 2002, p. 8). It's likely you are well versed in vision making and mission building (see the volume in this series on Cultural Leadership). The following are some best practices (suggestions) employed by principals I have had the pleasure to learn from that will serve as useful guides as you go about promoting your own vision, mission, and goals.

> *"The leader sets the goals, sets the priorities, and sets and maintains the standards."*
>
> —Peter Drucker

Ramsey (2003) highlights the importance of vision. He says, "There is no pat formula for vision building, but there are some insider secrets that can make it easier" (p. 144). He makes the following recommendations (I paraphrase):

1. Don't impose your vision. Inspire others around your vision for the school. Don't expect everyone to share your dreams for the school. Start small. Convene a group of interested parties. Word will spread soon enough. Ramsey (2003) wisely advises, "It's all right to leave some people behind. It happens every time a new journey is begun" (p. 144).

2. Think big; don't settle for mediocrity or complacency. If others share limiting views such as "these kids can't learn," ignore such prejudicial views. In fact, counter them with evidence and programs that prove them wrong. Always see the glass as half full. Set high goals for student learning and teacher work. Maintain high expectations for all who work in your school.

3. Think through all aspects of your vision. Some people will challenge your vision. If you have thought through your ideas for the future (e.g., sharing thoughts with a colleague or even a spouse helps), you will be better able to respond to limiting or contrary points of views.

4. Act like a blue-ribbon school even if your school is not one yet. It doesn't mean you have to be Polyannaish, just positive about your school's future. Your excitement will breed enthusiasm and participation from others.

5. Design a logo, a slogan, or a saying to represent your vision. Symbolism will go far toward reinforcing your vision.

6. Remain persistent. Despite setbacks or conflicts among personnel, stay the course and reinforce your commitment to your vision. Certainly, if you have no support for your vision, you may have to rethink your beliefs. A vision should be matched to context (i.e., school, community, etc.). It may not be the right vision for that particular school given, for instance, the experience levels of teachers who currently work in your school. Also, the timing might be off. Your vision might yield more positive response in a year or two.

7. Have others formally accept your vision. Develop a platform or vision statement. Have students, teachers, and parents refer to it in various ways (e.g., posters, lesson plans, PTA meetings).

8. Keep your vision organic, in the sense that it evolves to meet new realities or exigencies.

Your vision, therefore, should never be imposed. Your vision should be forward looking; reach for the stars. Think through your vision carefully. Maintain an upbeat outlook. Look for ways to publicize your vision. Remain flexible to alter your vision as situations demand.

> *"Those who would change school systems must think systematically."*
>
> —Phillip Schlechty

Visions that last are translated into mission statements that concretize the vision. A local high school vision statement, for instance, that seeks "to become a premier urban public high school recognized throughout the state for its diversity and excellence in mathematics and science" might frame a mission as follows: "To provide each student with advanced academic coursework in math and science so as to produce future leaders in urban communities." Another sample mission statement appears later in this chapter, in Section 5.

Strategic goals are statements that are framed to actualize the mission. Two goals for the mission and vision above might be framed as follows: Strategic priority goal #1: Develop infrastructure and support, including innovative technologies, that promote excellence in math and science teaching. Strategic priority goal #2: Develop and maintain collaborative ventures and partnerships within the local urban community so that students may undertake internships related to their work in math and sciences. Other sample goals are articulated later in this chapter.

Reflective Question

1. How can you inspire others around your vision?

---

3. CONDUCTING A SWOT ANALYSIS

The SWOT strategy or technique is very popular, easy to use, and a really simple and effective vehicle for planning strategically. Four broad categories or questions are framed:

S: What are the organization's internal Strengths?

W: What are the organization's internal Weaknesses?

O: What external Opportunities might move the organization forward?

T: What external Threats might hold the organization back?

The information that follows, in part, is retrieved from the Web site of the Alliance for Nonprofit Management (2003–2004c), a very useful Web site that should be explored in more depth.

SWOT analyses involve identifying key school constituents (e.g., teachers, paraprofessionals, or parents) and having them work through the SWOT strategy. According to the Alliance for Nonprofit Management (2003–2004c):

> Evaluating an organization's general strengths and weaknesses, as well as the strengths and weaknesses specific to each of its programs, typically includes assessments of:
> - staff and board capabilities,
> - quality of programs,
> - reputation of both the organization and individual programs,
> - management information and financial systems,
> - office facilities and equipment, etc.

Effective school organizations accentuate their strengths while minimizing and working on their weaknesses. "In other words, this process isn't just about fixing the things that are wrong, but also nurturing what is right" (Alliance for Nonprofit Management, 2003–2004c).

A similar approach should be taken in regard to your school's opportunities and threats. At this point in the SWOT strategy, you examine carefully "the external trends that influence the organization, [including] political, economic, social, technological, demographic, and legal . . . forces" (Alliance for Nonprofit Management, 2003–2004c).

> These external forces include such circumstances as changing client needs, increased competition, changing regulations, and so on. They can either help an organization move forward (opportunities) or hold an organization back (threats)—but opportunities that are ignored can become threats, and threats that are dealt with appropriately can be turned into opportunities. (Alliance for Nonprofit Management, 2003–2004c)

As principal, you would meet with each constituent group separately at first and work through the SWOT analysis, making certain to record all relevant information. Poster paper large enough for the entire group to see works well, and flipcharts are commonly used, too. Identify a coordinator to lead the group through the process while she or he records the information. Ideas are brainstormed and later sifted through to place all ideas in categories. A summary is made of each category. A similar pattern of activity is followed for each constituent group. A larger whole-group meeting of all constituents is planned as data are shared and discussed. Final data are organized and presented to whole-group discussion. Your assistant principals and you prepare the final analysis for schoolwide or board approval. The outcome becomes the essence of your strategic plan. Conducting these meetings collaboratively, with each person having a stake in participating and sharing views, fosters goodwill and acceptance of the plan even though some individuals might disagree with specific aspects.

Reflective Question

1. How might you use the SWOT analysis? Anticipate some opposition to its use and how you might counter claims against its use.

---

4. A GUIDE TO STRATEGIC PLANNING

Much literature discusses strategic planning. Many guidelines are provided. Some are useful, but many others are not. Section 4 of this chapter reviews some of the most useful information related to strategic planning. The information, in part, is drawn from an important article by Jan Lyddon (1999).

Although the information that follows is not drawn from schools, its relevance is nonetheless strong. Lyddon (1999), in her piece called "Strategic Planning in Smaller Nonprofit Organizations," first addresses the question "What is strategic planning?"

Most of us know that planning is a way of looking toward the future and deciding what the organization will do in the future. *Strategic planning* is a disciplined effort to produce decisions and actions that guide and shape what the organization is, what it does, and why it does it (Bryson, 1995). Both strategic planning and long-range planning cover several years. However, strategic planning requires the organization to examine what it is and the environment in which it is working. Strategic planning also helps the organization to focus its attention on the crucial issues and challenges. Therefore, it helps the organization's leaders decide what to do about those issues and challenges.

In short, as a result of a strategic planning process, an organization will have a clearer idea of what it is, what it does, and what challenges it faces. If it follows the plan, it will also enjoy enhanced performance and responsiveness to its environment.

After Lyddon (1999) argues for collaboration and wide input into the planning process, she makes the point that strategic planning should not be initiated in response to a current crisis. Deal with the crisis, she says. When waters have calmed a bit, begin the process. Some of the initial steps she suggests are:

- **List some of the main issues that face the organization.** This need not be a complete list, nor does it have to be fully organized. However, knowing some of the concerns of the organization will help those who will be asked to be involved in planning to prepare.

- **Set aside some time for the planning process.** Members of the board and staff who will be involved in planning should agree to take time for the planning process. This could involve a few hours a week for three to four weeks, or it could involve a single day or weekend. The plan writer, of course, will spend more time than others, because he or she will be preparing a document that represents decisions made at planning meetings. I recommend that the total time frame from starting the planning process to adopting the plan not stretch out for more than three months for a small organization.

- **Decide if a facilitator would be helpful.** Some organizations find that an individual who is not directly involved with the organization's regular work can help them with their planning process.

- **Find a place for the planning meetings to occur.** It is often helpful to meet somewhere other than the standard meeting location for the organization, because a different setting can help members of the group to step out of their usual patterns. The planning location should be comfortable, should include tables or other surfaces for participants to write on, and should have room to move around. Having the ability to provide refreshments for planning participants is also needed. Some organizations use large sheets of paper to record ideas, so having a planning location that permits hanging paper (using masking tape or other nondestructive adhesive) on the walls is ideal.

> *"The only goal worth talking about is transforming the current school system so that large-scale, sustainable, continuous reform becomes built in."*
>
> —Michael Fullan

Lyddon (1999) then outlines in some detail steps she considers important in the strategic planning process. She cautions readers to apply those steps that make the most sense for the particular organization. I have extracted only those steps I feel are most directly relevant to you as principal.

Step 1: Mission Review (approximate time required: 30–45 minutes)

Nearly every organization these days has a mission statement. It is helpful to periodically review the mission and to change it if necessary. An organization's mission is its reason for being, its purpose, or its social justification for existing. Just stating the organization's mission isn't enough. Clarifying the organization's purpose helps eliminate a great deal of unnecessary conflict and helps channel the organization's discussions and activity.

Suggested Method. Before the meeting begins, write the mission statement on an easel pad. Post the paper on the wall or an easel where everyone can see it. Ask someone in the group to read the mission aloud. Identify words or phrases that stand out and circle them. Then discuss each of the questions listed below, and write summarized responses to each on separate large sheets of paper. This is usually best done with the whole group participating.

The classic planning process begins by writing a mission statement. I recommend instead that the planning team members simply start by reviewing the mission statement, including asking the following questions to help them understand the mission better:

- Who are we? If the organization were walking down the street and someone asked who it was, what would the answer be? Distinguish what it is and what it does.
- In general, what are the basic social or political issues the organization exists to meet, or what are the basic social or political problems the organization exists to address? This is the basic social justification for the organization's existence.
- What, in general, does the organization do to recognize, anticipate, and respond to those needs or problems? How does the organization find out about them and decide what to do?
- Who are the key stakeholders for the organization, and how should we respond to them? How do we find out what they want from the organization?
- What are the organization's philosophy, values, and culture?
- What makes the organization unique or distinctive; that is, what gives the organization its competitive advantage?

Step 2: "Back to the Future" (approximate time required: 45–60 minutes)

In planning, we usually assume we are thinking only of the future. However, the organization's past is a source of much information about what has been effective and what has not. It is highly useful for the planning team to look backward for the same number of years it is expecting to plan into the future. For example, if the planning horizon is five years into the future, then look back over the previous five years.

> "What we call the beginning is often the end. To make an end is to make a beginning. The end is where we must start from."
>
> —T. S. Eliot

Suggested Method. Tape four large sheets of easel pad paper together (this should provide a sheet of about four by five feet). Using a strip of masking tape, mark a line horizontally across the middle of the large four-by-five-foot sheet. Across the top of the sheet, write the years (e.g., 2000, 2001, 2002, 2003, 2004). Give each participant a pad of four-by-six-inch Post-it notes and a pen or marker. Have the facilitator or leader then give instructions to the group to think about all of the organization's "highs" or "lows" that occurred in the past five years. Have each participant write silently, noting each event or incident on a separate Post-it. Be sure to mark the year on each Post-it. After a few minutes of writing, have the leader instruct the members of the group to start posting their notes on the sheet at the appropriate place along the line. The organization's "highs" go above the line, and the "lows" go below the line. The height of the Post-it notes above or below the line indicates just how high the "high" was or how low the "low" was.

Once the group members have completed this task, review the items. Usually the leader reads these aloud, perhaps asking for clarification on each.

Have the group discuss the items and look for themes among them. On a separate large easel pad sheet, note the themes. They might include funding levels (obtaining grants or losing them), arrival or departure of certain leaders, successful or unsuccessful management of crises. Asking questions such as the following can help clarify some of the issues:

- What opportunities has the organization had? How has the organization responded to these opportunities? (Has it taken

advantage of them? been unable to take advantage of them?
ignored them?)
- What threats has the organization had to deal with during this
  time period? Which were handled successfully, which unsuccess-
  fully, and which were ignored?
- What strengths did the organization rely on to deal with threats
  or opportunities? Which strengths did the organization ignore?
- What weaknesses has the organization had in dealing with
  threats and opportunities? What has the organization done
  about them?

Step 3: Envisioning the Future (approximate time required: 15–45 minutes)

At this stage, it is helpful to start looking briefly into the future of
the organization. This is an exercise requiring imagination, not necessarily "practical" ideas. However, this kind of exercise can often result
in some of the best ideas for an organization's future—along with some
of the wackiest!

Suggested Method. Have the group's leader ask each member to
imagine she or he has a friend who has been deeply involved in the
organization, but who has left the area and lost touch with the organization. However, five years later, this friend writes to the member and
asks the member about the organization. The member writes back to
his or her friend, describing in great detail what the organization is
doing. The member describes the activities and programs, the clients,
the organization's finances, and its staff and board. In short, the member describes what is happening. Have each member be as specific as
possible in writing the description on the notepads, but do not have the
members talk to one another. Spend about five minutes on this.

Then divide into groups of three to five people, and gather around
easels or large sheets of paper with the notes and draft letters to the
friends who have "left." Have members write their comments on the
large sheet of paper and discuss them among themselves. They may
want to list some of the common elements on each large sheet of paper
as well as to identify some of the unique or interesting ideas. Spend
about 10–15 minutes in small groups.

Have the group leader then use a "master" sheet of paper and ask
the first group to read its first item. Have the other groups that have
similar items cross them off their lists. Have the leader then put it on the
"master" list of common ideas. Keep going around the room in the

same manner. By the end, there should be a list of ideas that are common to two or more of the groups.

Next, have the group leader hand out five to eight sticky dots per person. Have the group members then vote on the items they like best by putting one dot on each item they like. They may vote on the "master" list or on the items remaining on the original sheets. The items receiving the most votes become higher-priority items for the group to consider when planning.

Step 4: SWOT (see Section 3 of this chapter)

Interested readers are referred to the Web site for good directive information on applying the SWOT analysis.

Step 5: Planning Themes (approximate time required: 30–60 minutes)

One of the first steps the organization should have taken in deciding to plan was listing some of the issues around which to plan. At this point in the planning process, the planning team will synthesize information from its earlier steps in planning and combine it with the issues or themes identified at the outset. This will form the basis for developing specific steps and tasks to implement the plan.

Suggested Method. In Step 3, Envisioning the Future, the planning team dreamed about the future and voted on the most important options to be considered. Once again, using the easel pad paper, list the items in descending order from the Envisioning the Future list. Next, review the SWOT analysis to identify the most important opportunities and strengths. List those on the large sheet of paper. At this point, some of the items from the SWOT list and the Envisioning the Future list may seem very similar. These similar items should be combined into a single item whenever possible. Through discussion among the members of the group, have the planning team come up with up to 10 issues or themes. However, there is no magic number of themes, and each planning team will have to decide for itself if the themes are distinct from one another or are too broad. Some questions the group might ask itself include the following:

- Is each issue or theme consistent with the organization's mission? If not, should the mission be changed or should the theme(s) be restated?

- Are the themes consistent with one another? It may seem obvious that the organization doesn't want to suggest, for example, expanding and contracting the same program at the same time, but it is easy to miss these contradictions.

• Are the themes or items distinct enough from one another that they can be easily categorized? For example, issues related to the physical plant or space occupied by the organization may be separated from issues related to the personnel of the organization. There may be interrelationships (e.g., more staff may require more space), but the themes should be listed separately. They will be linked later on in the process.

• Is anything missing? Conversely, is there too much? Sometimes planning teams are too caught up in the immediate issues, so they fail to see the larger picture, or they become too global and too general. One way to check whether anything is missing is to review the notes from all the previous steps in the planning process, including the issues originally set out by the organization. Also, the planning team might wish to check with the organization's board of directors at this point to ensure the themes are inclusive enough.

• Does everyone understand the items? A way of checking this is to ask individuals to quickly restate each theme in their own words.

Step 6: Setting Out the Steps and Time Frame (approximate time required: 60–120 minutes or longer)

Suggested Method. Using the themes developed in the previous step, list each on a separate easel pad sheet. Then, have the members of the planning team begin to brainstorm the major steps or components of each theme while the facilitator or leader writes them down. For example, if the organization identified its building as inadequate, and a theme for planning is replacing the building, some of the brainstormed steps might include investigating buying a new building versus renting more space and conducting a needs analysis for size and space usage. For some themes, there will be many items brainstormed, including some that will be contradictory. That's all right, because these contradictions will be resolved later on in the process. This stage is simply designed to flesh out the framework a bit.

Next, tape several large sheets of paper together and draw vertical lines on them to divide the years into the future (e.g., 2005, 2006, 2007, 2008, 2009). Label the years at the top of the large sheet.

Post the lists of planning themes and their major components near this large sheet so everyone can see them. Using large Post-it notes, have individual planning team members write components on separate Post-its. Individually, silently, have them begin to post the notes on the large sheet of paper within the year in which they believe the planning component or step should be largely *finished* or *resolved*. For example, if the organization needs more space, a team member might write "space needs analysis completed" on a Post-it and put it in the column for 2006. Another might write the same thing but put it in the column for 2005. Have the members also develop additional steps and post them on the large sheet. Once the group has slowed its pace of posting items, have the group leader then begin to discuss what is posted on the large sheet.

At this point, the process may become somewhat messy, and members of the planning team should feel free to move around, write on the large sheet, post more Post-its, move them around, and so on. Have the discussion focus on whether the steps are in the right order (e.g., one shouldn't prepare to move into a new building before signing the lease) and whether they can be accomplished in the time available. Also, having members identify interim steps (these can be listed with smaller-sized Post-its) is very useful at this point. Some groups may also use markers to draw lines between some of the Post-its and to add information to them (be sure the markers don't bleed through to the wall). Some of the items the group should consider include the following:

- Are the major steps in the "right" order?
- Are the completion dates realistic?
- Are there critical starting points and interim steps that should be listed?
- What are some of the linkages between the themes and their major components? Draw lines between these if necessary.
- How will we know when we have accomplished this objective? What will determine whether we have been successful?
- What are some of the weaknesses and threats that will affect the organization's ability to complete each step? How can they be dealt with, and are additional steps needed in order to ensure the organization can accomplish its goals?
- What resources (e.g., time, personnel, talent, and money) are needed to accomplish each component or step? Are these resources currently available to the organization, or must they be acquired? If they must be acquired first, then they should be identified in the appropriate place(s) on the large sheet of paper.

Most people are familiar with the structure of goals and objectives. What emerges from this stage of discussion is a set of goals (the themes) and objectives (the steps or components within each theme). Stating the objectives in action-oriented, time-delimited terms is very important. Organizations need to be able to measure their successes (and understand their failures) and state clearly what is to be done, by when, and by whom. This is, therefore, a very important component of the plan.

However, it is likely that there will be more objectives listed in the early years of the planning period than in the later years. This is fine, and as the organization moves through its planning cycle, it will add objectives to accomplish in future years.

If possible, provide different-colored Post-its for each theme area. Alternatively, mark horizontal lines on the large sheets of paper to separate the themes' steps or components from one another.

Step 7: Bringing It All Together—Writing the Plan (approximate time required: 20–60 hours)

The plan writer will have been taking careful notes throughout the process, including preparing interim reports between planning sessions. The plan writer now must assemble the information into a coherent document that reflects the key decisions of the planning team and enables the organization to move forward to implementation.

Suggested Method. The plan writer may wish to begin with a basic outline and prepare what amounts to minutes of each session or meeting of the planning team. The plan writer, however, should also add to the plan so that it becomes more than simply a set of minutes or a record of what occurred. The writer will need to insert some ideas and clarification into the plan. Following is a suggested outline for the final plan:

- The organization's mission. This section may also include any relevant comments summarizing some of the ways the organization's mission makes it unique or provides it a competitive advantage.
- The organization's mandates and its stakeholders
- A summary of the SWOT analysis
- Vision of success. This section may include descriptions of key items the planning team identified in its Envisioning the Future exercise. The plan writer may wish to modify the items on the list

somewhat so that it will be clear how the organization will know it is succeeding.

- Strategic issues, goals, and objectives. This section will be the meat of the plan, because within it will be a listing of each planning theme (now identified as a strategic issue) and the goals and objectives associated with it.
- Financial implications of the plan
- Time line for reviewing and updating the plan

Step 8: Reviewing and Revising the Mission (approximate time required: 30–60 minutes)

Early in the planning process, the organization's planning team reviewed the mission statement. At this later stage in the planning process, it is important to review the mission once again and to modify it to reflect the plans and ambitions of the organization. Sometimes a mission is too narrowly stated, and a strategic planning process may identify areas needing broader focus; conversely, a mission may be too vague, and it will need specifics.

Once the organization has a draft of a plan, it is helpful to review the mission with the plan in mind. If the items in the plan are out of sync with the mission, either the mission or the plan will need revision. Depending on the plan writer's capabilities, she or he may suggest some wording changes as a draft for revising the mission.

Suggested Method. Post the original statement of the mission (from Step 1) where the planning team can easily see it. Reread the mission aloud, noting those words or phrases identified earlier that raised questions or special interest. Next, review the planning themes (i.e., the strategic issues). Are there linkages between the strategic issues and the mission statement? Using a marker pen, add or delete items from the mission or from the strategic issues. More large easel pad sheets may be needed to accurately reflect the results of this discussion.

Once the planning team has prepared suggested changes to the organization's mission, the entire board must adopt the mission statement.

Step 9: Adopting the Plan (approximate time required: 30–45 minutes)

The planning team and the plan writer may have considered several drafts of the plan before presenting a final version to the board of directors. As a separate item at a regular board meeting, the plan should be formally presented to the board for its consideration and adoption. Ideally, the board members will have read the plan before the board meeting, but it is often helpful to provide a verbal overview of the plan's contents.

Step 10: Checking Progress on the Plan (approximate time required: 15–30 minutes)

Once the board has adopted the plan, it should also plan to check the progress on accomplishing the plan's goals and objectives. Such checkpoints should occur at regular board meetings, perhaps every three months. The time for checking may vary with the nature of the objectives, but their review should be an important part of the board's business on a regular basis.

Lyddon (1999) concludes with sage advice:

> Just as it is important to get started with planning, it is important to finish a planning process. In some ways, though, *effective* planning never ends because a plan must be revised and updated on a regular basis. Nonetheless, the planning process champion must ensure the planning process comes to a successful conclusion and that the organization can move to implementing the plan.

Reflective Question

1. How can Lyddon's steps assist you in setting up a strategic process in your school?

---

5. WEST MORRIS REGIONAL HIGH SCHOOL DISTRICT'S LONG-RANGE PLAN

Quite often an invaluable way to learn about strategic planning is to see a plan that was actually used by a school district. The 2000–2005 strategic plan initiative of the West Morris Regional High School District in Chester, New Jersey, is a good example of best practice. Fully understanding the enormous benefits of such a process, the district convened a planning committee. The district preferred to call the process a "long-range plan" instead of using the word *strategic*, to "emphasize that District goals would span time, would be clearly focused on success for all students, and would maintain a continuity of purpose" (West Morris Regional High School District, 2000–2005, p. 1). The planning committee established a "mission, a set of goals and strategies that would serve" to guide the whole process. In the words of forward-thinking Superintendent Kiernan, who emphasized the collaborative process and a focus on student achievement:

An important value of the long range planning process has been the collaborative efforts of many groups in the District and community. A shared understanding of the need for goal setting is extremely important to the quality of success for a long range plan. Research continues to show that high involvement of stakeholders leads to improved standards of success, not only for students, but also for overall District operations. We have seen this happen in the West Morris Regional High School District over the last five years with the first plan. Student achievement continues to improve, and the high standards of the District are recognized and honored by state and national agencies.

We take pride in the fact that the District has experienced many challenges and successes. However, the Board of Education and the staff have always operated with the belief that there is room to build upon and expand our success. In order to maintain a high quality school experience for every student, it is important to maintain the persistent focus and a consistent direction established by the District's mission.

Examine the excerpted material from their strategic plan, and complete the reflective exercise that follows.

Mission 2000–2005

The West Morris Regional High School community will provide students with an intellectually challenging experience that promotes a passion for learning, academic excellence, involved citizenship, and personal responsibilities. This experience will foster the development of creative, confident, compassionate, and resilient individuals.

Goals 2000–2005

1. All students will create and periodically assess a personal development plan that will include challenging academic goals, extracurricular activities, and community service.

2. Each year, students will demonstrate increasing levels of academic achievement by meeting rigorous district standards facilitated through dialogue among all educational institutions ranging from elementary through postsecondary.

3. All students will participate in activities that foster involvement, cooperation, and personal responsibility and that value the worth of others within the school and extended community.

4. The West Morris Regional community will ensure a stimulating, progressive, and challenging learning environment that meets the rigorous standards and educational demands of a changing global society.

5. Students will become active critical thinkers whose ability to work collaboratively and integrate interdisciplinary knowledge will promote practical life skills and a lifelong passion for learning.

Goals, Strategies, and Objectives

Goal 1

Strategy:

We will design and implement a personal development planning process that will be continually revised throughout the student's high school career.

Objective:

Implement a program that allows each student to develop a comprehensive, curriculum-based, personal developmental plan.

Goal 2

Strategies:

- We will establish departmental committees composed of members from all relevant institutions, ranging from elementary through postsecondary, to facilitate curriculum coordination.
- We will continue to pursue academic excellence through an ongoing investigation and refinement of our educational programs.

Objectives:

- Establish horizontal articulation among those who share common teaching responsibilities.
- Establish vertical articulation within specific departments in the high school for the purpose of curriculum alignment and clarification of goals and expectations.
- Construct vertical articulation with the sending districts (K–12) to achieve curriculum alignment.
- Enhance ongoing articulation with colleges and universities to prepare students for the transition from high school to college.
- Provide curricular leadership and vision through established positions and continuous training.

Goal 3

Strategy:

We will identify the skills inherent in an involved, responsible, and cooperative individual and integrate them into a program that supports student participation within the school and extended community.

Objectives:

- Support a staff development plan that enhances student involvement, cooperation, and personal responsibility and that values the worth of others within the school and extended community.
- Design curriculum strategies that promote skills associated with cooperation, responsibility, involvement, and valuing the worth of others.
- Encourage all students to participate in the total school and extended community.
- Promote community awareness of the goals of our extracurricular program, which are to foster involvement, responsibility, cooperation, and valuing the worth of others.

Goal 4

Strategy A:

We will create, with community support, a collaborative process to: (a) assess the current status and use of the facilities and technology; (b) project future educational requirements (2, 5, and 10 years out); and (c) develop and execute a plan to meet those needs.

Objectives:

- Provide the necessary data to compare the current capacity to the future demands of the district.
- Determine the necessary data to project the impact of mandates, standards, and curriculum on the facilities.
- Recommend changes to the facilities that will meet future needs.
- Provide the community with a final plan for changes to the facilities.

Strategy B:

We will provide a safe and secure environment that promotes the development of a student's personal, social, and emotional well-being.

Objectives:
- Ensure that all students are well informed, self-confident, and open in their communication with school personnel and are comfortable raising issues and asking for help.
- Guarantee a strong atmosphere of community and a climate of respect, ownership, and pride in our district, where every student feels included and is involved as a contributing member of the school community.
- Recognize that a supportive relationship exists between students and guidance/support services personnel and that each grade level is acknowledged for its collective set of challenges, strengths, and opportunities.
- Guarantee that harassment of any kind is not tolerated and that all school personnel are proactive and vigilant in recognizing and responding to all incidents of harassment.
- Encourage all students to follow a standard conduct that nurtures productive behavior and clearly indicates consequences for behavior that interferes with another's right to learn.
- Ensure that district athletic programs provide a culture and a process that are inclusive and fair-minded and that maintain the self-esteem of each student.
- Maintain a district crisis management/security plan that is current, comprehensive, and operational.

Goal 5

Strategy:

We will develop a plan to support an interdisciplinary curriculum that fosters critical thinking, includes multiple methods of assessment, and culminates in a project incorporating life skills and demonstrating a passion for knowledge.

Objectives:
- Establish a senior project as a graduation requirement.
- Establish an interdisciplinary curriculum.

Reflective Questions

1. How does this plan inform your practice as a building principal?
2. What aspects or ideas of the plan have prompted you to consider ways of improving your school?
3. How does this plan help the high school go about its work strategically?

CONCLUSION

In this chapter, you have been introduced to some successful planning strategies, the importance of visioning, tips for conducting SWOT analyses, a sample guide to strategic planning, and one high school district's long-range plan. Systemic reform requires principals to exhibit strategic leadership skills. These principals strategize constantly and make strategic choices. We see that strategic leaders must have a thorough understanding of their schools. Heck and Weiss (2005) highlight several key aspects of strategic leadership that are useful and relevant for school principals, although they discuss leaders in general. Some of their views include the following:

- *Principals have a vision and know how to achieve it.* Heck and Weiss (2005) say, "A vision for effective teaching and learning is not enough . . . strategic leaders possess a larger view of reform and a road map for getting there" (p. 4).
- *Principals cultivate broad understanding and support for their vision.* Strategic leaders possess keen collaborative skills and reach out to relevant constituencies within and outside of the school.
- *Principals cultivate commitment to their vision.* Strategic leaders are persistent advocates for excellence at all levels, and they continually urge others to systematically work together to design effective learning environments for all students.
- *Principals use interventions to translate their vision into reality.* Strategic leaders live by the saying "actions speak louder than words" (p. 7).
- *Principals start small, refine their strategies as needed, and provide evidence that their strategies are succeeding.*

"All good things begin with a sound plan" is probably a good motto for the principal who serves as strategic leader.

CHAPTER THREE

Best Practices in Data-Driven Decision Making

"Data cannot make decisions but decisions must be data-based."

—John H. Hansen and Elaine Liftin

"Evaluation involves not only looking at the outcomes or impact of a program but also documenting the process and progress of the program."

—Olatokunbo S. Fashola

"The leadership cadre at a school must pursue means to measure student achievement other than through standardized tests."

—John H. Hansen and Elaine Liftin

Effective principals use data to inform their curricular and instructional decisions schoolwide. In the "old" days, however, such data were limited to the yearly standardized test, usually given in late spring. Today, in the era of heightened accountability and, more important, in light of our deeper and more sophisticated notions of assessment (Popham, 2001), testing is varied and is considered only a part of the overall assessment system in place in a given school. Principals cull data from a variety of sources: standardized tests in various content areas, teacher-made tests, project-based learning activities, portfolios, surveys, and so forth. Long gone is the day when a principal made a decision in isolation of sufficient and rigorous data. It is commonly held today that "in a world of accountability, principals must be leaders in collecting and analyzing data to shape decisions that lead to continuous improvement" (P. G. Young, 2004, p. 96). As principal in the 21st century, you are likely expected by school board members and region or district office administrative leaders to possess knowledge and skills in data analysis and interpretation. You are required to use such data to inform your decision making in order to best promote student achievement for all students.

As a data-driven principal, you:

- Are suspicious of people who advocate a position or change without data to back up a decision
- Request teachers and others to reaffirm their decisions, instructional or otherwise, with data that are varied, pointing to a clear trend
- Spend time looking over trend data over time (e.g., student attendance rates, teacher absentee rates, standardized test scores—disaggregated or aggregated over time)
- Collect data via questionnaires, for instance, to assess parental and student satisfaction and use such data to make some key decisions
- Always base major decisions on data that have been collected from a variety of sources, analyzed, interpreted, and shared
- Create a culture of improvement and a learning community

"Get and use data to argue for your positions and to demonstrate the success, or failure, of policy."

—Nicholas M. Michelli

This chapter will highlight some varied ways you as the principal can achieve these aforementioned ideals. Consult the Best Resources section of this volume for references that treat this important subject in greater depth.

What You Should Know About Data-Driven Decision Making

- **Learning From Role Models**—Exemplary practices of real principals are highlighted.
- **Using Data to Empower**—Shaver's (2004) guidelines for using data to make decisions are highlighted and expanded upon.
- **Collecting Data**—Primary and secondary ways of collecting data to inform your decision making are discussed.
- **Easy Steps to Program Evaluation**—Five steps you can use to evaluate programs are reviewed.

---

1. LEARNING FROM ROLE MODELS

This first best practice discussion is culled from the work of three principals I have observed over the past several years. These principals, in my view, represent good role models for our discussion about data-driven decision making. Each of them voices a strong commitment to improving their schools, and they have created a culture of improvement within the context of a learning community that represents best practice. Discussion of what they do and their strategies is highlighted without revealing potentially sensitive information about them or their schools. Also, I have compiled their approaches into a case study of one, fictionalized principal. As a new principal, you may learn about them by reading about some of the strategies they employ. I have culled strategies that have been acknowledged by others in their schools and districts that represent best practice. I have also observed their work, albeit from a distance. The information presented in the bulleted list that highlighted what data-driven principals do was actually culled from observing and learning about what these principals have done and do. Their work is instructive. Specific strategies or activities are explicated below in such a way as to make them easily accessible and understandable. I have not provided a richer, more detailed context for the work of each of these principals because of space limitations, besides the fact that my purpose in this work is aimed at relaying easy-to-learn, more prescriptive ideas and strategies so that you may readily incorporate them. I intend, at a later date, to write an article about these principals and their work in case study fashion with more depth and discussion.

Katica Sanchez became principal of a school in a "rough" section of town. Low expectations, inexperienced and often unlicensed teachers (i.e., teachers teaching out of license or on a substitute, per diem basis) comprised the majority of faculty, low pass rates on standardized reading and math tests, and a culture of despair characterized, in part, the educational landscape of this middle school. Resistance from the more experienced teachers and an uninformed, inactive parent body made Sanchez's work an uphill struggle. Yet, as a newly assigned principal with a firm commitment to improve her school and student learning, Ms. Sanchez was resolute in her approach to changing the "culture of failure and mediocrity," as she called it, "that prevails in this school." Again, without detailing her herculean efforts in a relatively short time (three years), below are some of the beliefs, strategies, and activities she employed, centered primarily around the topic under discussion in this chapter. The information that follows is meant to serve as best practice for you and as a guide to your own practice as a principal.

• She employed best practices as detailed in other volumes in this Principal Series, particularly cultural, instructional, and collaborative leadership.

• Ms. Sanchez was the perennial optimist. People described her as "upbeat . . . always seeing the glass half full . . . always looked for the good in people, . . . believing that people want to be liked and do a good job." She saw her role as facilitating best practices among teachers. She accentuated the best in people. She was an articulate and dynamic speaker who used every opportunity to share her vision of excellence for all people, teachers, staff, and students. Someone in the school community commented, "She is someone I admire because she 'walks her talk.'"

• The previous bullet should not imply that she was a pushover. She had high expectations for performance and would chastise people, "always in private," if she felt they weren't meeting her expectations or "doing their best."

• She expected all the students to achieve their best. She was "results oriented," as one of her assistant principals commented. "She expects each of us, administrators and teachers alike, to demonstrate that what we do 'makes a difference.'" "She expects us to provide concrete evidence that our efforts are yielding results. Just saying it was effective doesn't cut it with her. She wants evidence."

• She talks about student achievement all the time. Every faculty meeting and most memoranda she issues are focused on ways and opportunities to promote student learning that eventuate in achievement. She often says, "The bottom line: Are our students learning and achieving?"

• Although she focuses on achievement, she doesn't stress standardized assessment measures exclusively, although she considers them important. She accepts, solicits, and encourages data from a variety of informal and more formal assessment instruments such as questionnaires, interviews, and portfolio work. "She is fair in her approach to assessment, not relying on a single measure alone to demonstrate student achievement."

• She has created an atmosphere in which learning occurs and is expected by everyone. School secretaries and even custodial staff can "weigh in on student performance including social development issues" (i.e., behavioral patterns). She constantly asks everyone, "Well, what have we learned today?" and "How can we prove it or demonstrate it?" She encourages risk taking, especially in regard to instructional and curricular matters. "She is not afraid of us failing at times." She says, "We learn more from our mistakes than from our successes." "The pressure is off," one experienced teacher commented, "we can go ahead and teach in an atmosphere of encouragement and support without fear of reprisals or denigration."

• She places a suggestion box outside the main office so that anyone can drop in an anonymous comment. "I know she reads the comments because she refers to them at faculty meetings and suggests ways to address various concerns."

• She administers a questionnaire to teachers, parents, and students and summarizes the results at various forums. She asks, "What do the data suggest?" "How might we make any changes based on these findings?" In one case, for instance, parent responses indicated that parents who work out of the home would like to receive e-mailed updates on student projects. Rather than mandating that teachers now add on the burden of e-mailing parents on a daily basis, she asks, "What do these data suggest?" She leads a lively discussion "allowing us, actually, umm . . . empowering us to come up with solutions or ideas to address this parental concern." In the end, many teachers concur that e-mailed updates to parents are warranted and, in the long run, will enhance parental involvement, thus reducing student behavior problems and, most important, promoting higher rates of completion of homework assignments.

- She focuses on instruction in the classroom at every opportunity. She takes her role as instructional leader seriously and sees a strong, necessary connection between this role and pupil achievement. "She engages teachers in instructional dialogue and meaningful supervision (not evaluation). . . . She gets out of her office into the classrooms and saves report writing for downtimes and after school." "She strives to encourage good pedagogy and teaching. . . . Faculty and grade meetings focus almost exclusively on instructional issues." "She avoids quick-fix approaches that presumably guarantee high student achievement. . . . She knows that no instructional panaceas exist." "Although she certainly feels the increased pressure to raise student achievement, she goes about her work methodically, facilitating and supporting teachers in the classroom while, at the same time, expecting teachers to demonstrate and ensure student learning." She allows teachers to demonstrate such learning in a variety of ways: (a) pre- and posttest assessments in various curriculum areas, before and after each unit of instruction; (b) in lieu of formal observations, action research projects conducted over the course of the school year that focus on ways students are learning and achieving; (c) bulletin board displays; (d) classroom newsletters and papers that showcase, for instance, samples of student writing; (e) portfolio development projects over the course of a term or year showcasing progress in a variety of subject areas; and (f) videotaping of lessons and analyzing instructional procedures that point to specific in-class practices that promote student achievement (e.g., effective use of wait time, prompting, and probing techniques). Teachers share the varied ways they demonstrate student achievement at grade and faculty conferences.

- Ms. Sanchez utilizes action research to better understand her work and even solve specific instructional problems. She knows that action research, properly used, can have immeasurable benefits:

  o Creates a systemwide mind-set for school improvement
  o Fosters a professional problem-solving ethos
  o Enhances decision making
  o Promotes reflection and self-improvement
  o Instills a commitment to continuous instructional improvement
  o Creates a more positive school climate in which teaching and learning are foremost concerns

     o Empowers those who participate and promotes professional development

    She possesses much knowledge about action research. She realizes that action research is an ongoing process of reflection that involves four basic cyclical steps:

1. Selecting a Focus
   a. Know what you want to investigate.
   b. Develop some initial questions.
   c. Establish a plan to answer or better understand these questions.

2. Collecting Data
   a. Primary

      Questionnaires

      Observations

      Interviews

      Tests

      Focus groups

   b. Secondary

      School profile sheets

      Multimedia

      Portfolios

      Records

      Others

3. Analyzing and Interpreting Data

4. Taking Action

    • Because Ms. Sanchez is such an advocate of action research and data-based decision making, she challenges her assistant principals and teachers to make adjustments to their practices based on data collected and analyzed. "Evidence-based decision making is a necessity in today's educational world," she says, "and we must hold teachers and ourselves accountable for the work we do." She collaborates with teachers to review trend data that show student progress in reading comprehension, for example. "What do the data tell us? How can we use this information to change our practices in order to promote student achievement?" She encourages the use of varied data sources to draw conclusions. She summarizes her data on reading achievement, for instance, in the following table:

Instrument	Standard	Percentage meeting	Conclusion
Standardized reading achievement test	75% above 60th percentile	65% above 60th percentile (10% decrease over previous year); only 15% of ELL scored above norm	Expectation not met; examine achievement of ELL (speak with ESL teachers, supervisors, etc.)
Teacher-designed reading comprehension tests	75% above 60th percentile	85% above 60th percentile; 45% of ELL scored above norm	Expectation met, but why the difference compared to standardized tests?
Reading portfolios	At least 70% scoring "acceptable" on portfolio rubric	75% scored acceptable, but only 15% for ELL	Expectation met overall, but examine achievement for ELL
Monthly teacher-made exams	At least 50% scoring "acceptable" on writing rubric for idea development, sentence structure, and grammar	80% scored acceptable, but significantly less for girls	Expectation met overall, but examine achievement for girls
Student, teacher, parent surveys	At least 85% registering satisfaction with new approach to reading that incorporates a balanced literacy approach	90% approval rating among students and parents, but only 50% for teachers	Expectation not fully met; further study needed

This chart is shared with others in order to draw conclusions that might inform practice.

• Ms. Sanchez engages in reflective practice as a process by which she takes the time to contemplate and assess the efficacy of programs, practices, and personnel in order to make judgments about their appropriateness or effectiveness so that improvements or refinements might be achieved. She is a research-oriented leader who has a vision that guides her work. As she plans and works to improve her school, she collects and analyzes data to better inform her decisions. As a research-oriented leader, she is engaged in ongoing self-study in which she assesses the needs of her school, identifies problem areas, and develops strategies for becoming more effective.

As a reflective practitioner who values critical inquiry, she poses some of these questions, among others:

1. What concerns me?

2. Why am I concerned?

3. Can I confirm my perceptions?

4. What mistakes have I made?

5. If I were able to do it again, what would I do differently?

6. What are my current options?

7. What evidence can I collect to confirm my feelings?

8. Who might be willing to share their ideas with me?

9. What have been my successes?

10. How might I replicate these successes?

11. How can I best promote instructional improvement and raise student achievement?

12. In what other ways might I improve my school?

For Ms. Sanchez, reflection is the heart of professional practice.

Reflective Question

1. One principal referred me to the work of Hansen and Liftin (1999), in which I noted that the authors identified the following data sets:
   - Racial and gender distribution of school personnel
   - Age, degree, and certification distribution of school personnel
   - Percentage of school room and facility utilization
   - Percentage of students bused, on free and reduced lunch, and new to the district in the previous 12 months
   - Test scores by subject, subtests, and grade level for a three-year period (by class, race, limited English proficiency status, and other groups of significant size, if possible)
   - Attendance, behavioral, suspension, and dropout statistics for a three-year period
   - Mobility percentages for the school
   - Budget and other financial support for a three-year period
   - Graduation and completion rates for school
   - Record of the school's students in subsequent schools
   - Racial and gender distribution of student body
   - Attendance history of school personnel
   - Socioeconomic data on community
   - Racial, language, and school histories of students who will attend the school within one to five years

How might you use such data sets (trend data) to inform your decision making?

"Evaluation conducted at the school level can improve the quality of information used to make management, program, and instructional decisions."

—Joan L. Herman and Lynn Winters

2. USING DATA TO EMPOWER

According to Heidi Shaver (2004),

When data are collected and analyzed by teams or department members on a regular basis, they become a powerful vehicle not only for prompting individuals to make instructional changes, but also to take hold of the reins with a new-found sense of purpose and design their own destiny in the classroom. (p. 103)

Advocating a systematic approach to data-driven decision making, Shaver highlights four tasks of a principal as strategic leader:

1. Establish an assessment data system. Set up both a general and a subject- or area-specific assessment system. Familiarize yourself with various forms of data that could be used to inform faculty about student progress in academic and other areas. Track student data by examining enrollment figures, absentee and tardiness charts, percentages of students on grade level in major content areas as assessed by state standardized examinations, district or school profile sheets, and so forth. The assessment system should include performance-based activities. Use data to inform instructional decision making. On these last two points, see the two quotations that follow.

On Assessment

> "If you want to determine if students can write, have them write something. If you want to determine if students can operate a machine, have them operate a machine. If you want to determine if students can conduct an experiment, have them conduct an experiment. In short, if you want to determine if they can perform a task, have them perform the task."

> —Norman E. Gronlund

> "The aim of assessment is primarily to educate and improve student performance, not merely to audit it."

> —Grant Wiggins

An assessment system should take into consideration that learning is complex, multidimensional, integrated, and revealed in performance over time. Assessment is a goal-oriented process that works best when the programs it seeks to improve have clear, explicitly stated purposes. Assessment is tied to our student learning outcomes but also and equally to the experiences that lead to those outcomes.

Assessment is not just a department responsibility but a communitywide (internally and externally) responsibility. Assessment should be valued because you care about change and improvement. Ultimately, we are cognizant of our responsibility to our students and the public at large. The school's assessment system is multidimensional, ongoing, and cyclical in that data are used in formative and summative ways for decisions with respect to the students and for meaningful programmatic change in the curriculum. Assessments are also derived from internal and external sources. See Figure 3.1 for a general schematic flow chart to help guide an assessment system. Table 3.1, which follows, is just a

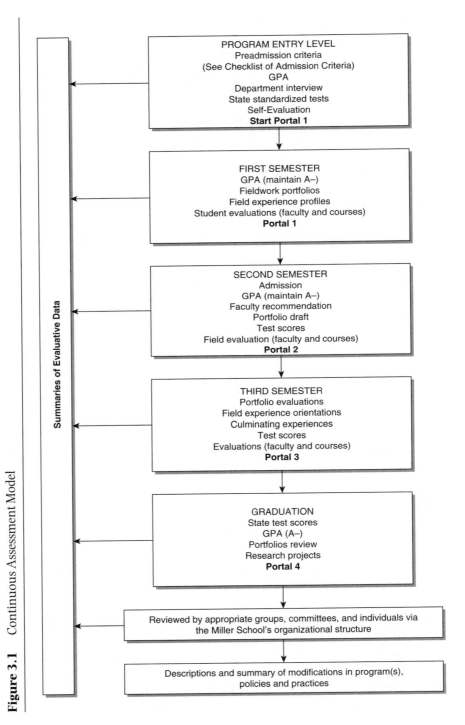

Figure 3.1 Continuous Assessment Model

Summaries of Evaluative Data

PROGRAM ENTRY LEVEL
Preadmission criteria
(See Checklist of Admission Criteria)
GPA
Department interview
State standardized tests
Self-Evaluation
Start Portal 1

FIRST SEMESTER
GPA (maintain A–)
Fieldwork portfolios
Field experience profiles
Student evaluations (faculty and courses)
Portal 1

SECOND SEMESTER
Admission
GPA (maintain A–)
Faculty recommendation
Portfolio draft
Test scores
Field evaluation (faculty and courses)
Portal 2

THIRD SEMESTER
Portfolio evaluations
Field experience orientations
Culminating experiences
Test scores
Evaluations (faculty and courses)
Portal 3

GRADUATION
State test scores
GPA (A–)
Portfolios review
Research projects
Portal 4

Reviewed by appropriate groups, committees, and individuals via
the Miller School's organizational structure

Descriptions and summary of modifications in program(s),
policies and practices

Table 3.1 Miller Middle School Assessment System

Assessment points at critical stages	Standards/ outcomes	Benchmarks	Assessment tools: internal (I) and external (E) measures	Aggregated data responsibility	Admission criteria
Entry into eighth grade	Content knowledge and skills	Passed seventh-grade exit exams in each content area GPA B+ or higher plus complete transcript review	Transcripts (E) Grade-level test scores (I) Interview (I)	Office of Admissions and Assessment Task Force (ATF)	Applicants admitted based on department criteria
Portal 1	Content knowledge and skills/ dispositions	Laboratory and experiential learning assignments	Passing score on rubric (26 or higher)	Course instructor ATF	Candidates assessed based on rubric (or *above standards*; *approaching standards* (conditional admittance); or *below standard* (rejection or alternate arrangements)
Portal 2	Content knowledge	Portfolio project	Passing score on rubric (12 or higher)	Composite score among thesis advisor, reader 1, and reader 2 ATF	Candidates assessed based on rubric (or *above standards*; *approaching standards* (conditional admittance); or *below standard* (rejection or alternate arrangements)

Note: Miller Middle School is a school for gifted students in mathematics and sciences. This chart provides a schematic overview of the assessment system for eighth graders in mathematics and science.

section of the more detailed assessments that can occur at various portals or stages. It, too, serves as a guide, albeit more specific.

Shaver's (2004) remaining three tasks of a principal are straight-forward.

2. Establish a formal, ongoing mechanism to report regularly to faculty, staff, parents, and so forth. As principal, you might set up quarterly reports that include summaries of assessment student data. Similar reports to parents are made at open meetings or via memoranda or e-mail communications.

3. Have the school leadership team analyze data and set goals. Heritage and Chen (2005) emphasize the importance of data analysis, commenting, "Effective action depends on the capacity of teachers and administrators to analyze data accurately and to infer a reasonable next step" (p. 709). "Merely collecting data in descriptive fashion does not move us forward. Through data analysis and interpretation we now understand why students, for instance, achieved at the levels they did" (p. 709). We may now know why third-grade female students, for instance, performed significantly higher in writing assessments than boys in the same grade. "After comprehensive data analysis, the next step in the process of investigation is to identify priorities and set goals for school improvement" (p. 710). These goals must be "measurable, time-sensitive, focused on student achievement, linked to assessment, written in clear language, realistic, and achievable" (Schmoker, 1999, as cited in Heritage & Chen, 2005, p. 710). A goal, for instance, in response to the example just described might be stated as "to increase writing proficiency among third-grade boys by 15% by the end of the next academic year."

4. Share goals, instructional strategies, and further assessment tools and criteria. Data-driven decision making is a schoolwide goal and enterprise. It certainly takes "a village" to raise student achievement. No one person can do it alone, because learning and achievement are complicated, nonlinear processes that involve the unified actions of many, as well as varied strategies and activities.

Reflective Question

1. How does the information presented in this section empower principals?

3. COLLECTING DATA

Sure, we are all committed to improving our schools. We are even in favor of using data to drive the decisions we may make, for instance, to develop different instructional strategies that raise student test scores. Further, we even realize that data collection is critical to our ability to do so. But how can we collect varied data? What types of data might we use to facilitate our decision making? And how might we or our assistants design such instruments for data collection? The information below is drawn, in part, from a chapter I've written on data collection (Glanz, 2003). Refer to that work for more detailed information on the entire research process, which is so integral to data-driven decision making.

Data collection must be varied, not emanating from merely one or two sources. Triangulating data, therefore, is imperative (i.e., culling data from at least three sources). Primary and secondary data sources are reviewed below.

Primary Data Collection Techniques

Questionnaires

Questionnaires are one of the most common types of data collection instruments (or data sources). Their ease of use and uncomplicated methods of data analysis make questionnaires an invaluable means of collecting data.

A questionnaire surveys respondents' attitudes toward a particular issue. Educational leaders may distribute questionnaires to assess attitudes of students, parents, teachers, or even other supervisors about a variety of issues, such as school climate and instructional supervision.

Sometimes, ready-made questionnaires that have been developed by companies are available for use. For example, the National Association of Secondary School Principals (NASSP, 1987) has developed several useful, ready-made questionnaires surveying school climate and teacher, student, and parent attitudes toward school. Also, you can call 800-228-0752 for the School Effectiveness Questionnaire, which can be hand tabulated or computer analyzed. In many cases, however, questionnaires may not be available to suit your unique needs. In such cases, you might have to construct your own questionnaire. See the discussion that follows on questionnaire construction.

Two types of questionnaires are most common: closed ended and open ended. Open-ended questionnaires include questions that allow

> "Program evaluation projects provide educators with the information and insights they need to refine and improve the services and programs they provide to their students. And that is a worthy goal."
>
> —Edward A. Brainard

respondents to elaborate on a given question. A questionnaire, for instance, composed of questions to ascertain a teacher's attitude toward supervision may include the following open-ended question: "Can you provide an example of a situation or experience in which you have benefited from supervision? Explain."

Note that although questionnaires are usually data collection instruments used in quantitative approaches, the responses to open-ended questions in questionnaires can be seen and interpreted as qualitative data. Very often, comments generated from open-ended questions can prove very useful and even crucial in determining such things as the value of the program under study.

Closed-ended questionnaires, on the other hand, do not allow respondents to elaborate; rather, they structure respondents' answers to predetermined choices. One of the most commonly used closed-ended questionnaires is known as the Likert scale. Many of us have taken a Likert-scale questionnaire at one time or another. Right? You recall those choices it gives, such as *strongly agree, agree, disagree,* and *strongly disagree*? A Likert scale is relatively easy to construct and easy to analyze. Below are some guiding principles to follow in constructing such scales:

1. Limit the number of items to as few as possible (ideally between 15 and 20 items). Long surveys are unlikely to be completed by respondents.

2. Avoid ambiguously worded statements. Construct items so that they will be interpreted in the same way by every respondent. Why is the following statement worded ambiguously?

"How often do you observe your fifth-grade teachers?"

rarely   *sometimes*   *often*

Right. What is meant by *observe?* A casual look; an in-depth, hour-long observation period; or some time in between? Moreover, what do the choices mean? How often is "sometimes"? Once a month, twice a month, or once a year?

Sometimes statements are phrased ambiguously because of sentence structure problems. Have a colleague or potential respondent proofread your items for ambiguity.

3. Avoid leading questions; that is, don't suggest that one response will be more appropriate than another. For example, avoid using a question such as "Don't you agree that peer coaching is marvelous?"

4. Avoid sensitive questions to which respondents may not reply honestly. For example, don't ask: "Have you always acted so ethically?"

5. Statements should be concise, not overly lengthy.

6. Develop objectives before you write the items (see examples in the sample questionnaire that follows).

7. Questionnaires should include statements that are conceptually related. If you are surveying attitudes of teachers toward bilingual education, then an example of a conceptually unrelated item would be: "I get along with my supervisor." This statement has little, if anything, to do with the major purpose of your questionnaire. One way to ensure that items are conceptually related is to match each item with your objectives. Does each item address one of the stated objectives?

8. Avoid response sets. Sometimes respondents will not actually read the survey but will merely go down a column circling all the *strongly disagree* choices. To avoid response sets, you must word half the items positively and half negatively. Placement of positively and negatively worded statements should be random. Don't intentionally place an item in the order you think is best. As long as about half of the items are positive statements and the other half are negative statements, and the items are randomly distributed, you will have avoided the response set problem.

Below is an example of two statements, one positively worded and the other in the negative:

Directions: Circle the response that best indicates the extent to which you agree or disagree with each statement below, where

    SA = Strongly Agree
     A = Agree
     D = Disagree
    SD = Strongly Disagree

SA   A   D   SD   1. Math is my favorite class.

SA   A   D   SD   2. Learning math is a waste of time.

If someone really enjoys math, she will circle *SA* for the first item and *SD* for the second. If the respondent circles *SA* for both items, you might have a response set. Too many response sets affect the validity and reliability of your questionnaire.

9. Prepare the cover letter. A cover letter should be brief and neat. The letter should explain the purpose of your study, emphasize its importance, give the respondent a good reason for completing the survey, and ensure the respondent's anonymity.

10. Field-test your survey to ensure consensual validity.

For a Likert-scale questionnaire, your objectives would be determined prior to developing the items. Note that your objectives would not be shared with respondents.

For more information about questionnaire construction, consult the following excellent references: Fink and Kosecoff (1998) and Thomas (1999). On survey validity and reliability, see Litwin (1995). For a comprehensive resource containing a collection of many easy-to-use assessment tools, see Bum and Payment (2000).

Observation

Another very common way to collect data is to observe and record information. Observations, in general, may take place in four ways:

1. *As a participant*—You may conceal your role when gathering data. For example, you, a principal, may want to study interactions among fellow principals at a conference. You are able to observe firsthand social interactions among principals. Being actively engaged in the conference affords you firsthand experience and data. Yet the ethics of concealing your purpose in interacting with others should be considered.

2. *As an observer-participant*—Your purpose is known by all participants. You may record data as they occur. Yet participants may be reluctant to share information if they know that what they will say or do will be recorded.

3. *As a participant-observer*—Your observation role is secondary to the participant role. You record data; however, you may not attend to all data.

4. *As an observer*—You observe without participating. Recording data can be accomplished without distractions, yet those being observed may feel uncomfortable with your sole role as observer.

Regardless of the way you collect data through observation, several key questions should be kept in mind (thanks to my colleague Dr. Barry Friedman, a former principal in the New York City Public Schools, for suggesting these questions):

1. What is the purpose of the observation?

2. Which individuals, events, settings, and circumstances are the focus of the investigation?

3. How are students, teachers, parents, and administrators behaving?

4. What activities are occurring?

5. How would you describe the social interaction?

6. How do people talk to each other?

7. What is the impact of my presence as an observer?

8. What instruments am I using to record data (e.g., pencil/paper, camera, video recorder, audio recorder)?

Two ways of collecting data through observation are particularly useful. First, written descriptions are most often employed by educational leaders when collecting data. For instance, when you observe a teacher, you may record information by taking field notes or "thick descriptions." Taking field notes is a convenient and simple way of recording observations. Although field notes are subject to observer bias and subjectivity, recording data anecdotally (without drawing conclusions or making value judgments) is acceptable for data collection. Still, this method of recording data is incomplete in the sense that it is impossible to record all events during a given lesson, for instance. Observations are therefore necessarily limited and should rarely be used as a *sole* means of collecting data.

A second way of collecting data through observation is preparing a checklist of some sort to facilitate observations. A checklist allows you to record instances of a particular behavior or practice. The checklist technique defines certain behaviors or events that can be checked off as they occur during a lesson, for example. Let's say that you are observing a teacher and want to keep a tally of the number of instances in which the teacher "gave directions," "praised," "criticized," "probed," and "asked questions" during a 15-minute segment of a lesson. Your checklist might look something like the one in Table 3.2 (culled from Sullivan & Glanz, 2005). Checklists such as this one can assist in the

Table 3.2   English-Language Learners

Accommodation or modification	Was this element present? Yes No N/A	What is the evidence?
Teacher talk is modified: slower speech; careful choice of words, idioms, and expressions		
Teacher allows wait time and monitors teacher input versus student output		
Definitions and language are embedded in content or context		
Real-world artifacts present that support comprehension		
Elicit and draw on students' backgrounds to build prior knowledge		
Teacher uses nonverbal cues to support comprehension		

Class:

Date:

Time:

systematic collection of data through observation. See Sullivan and Glanz (2005) for a variety of similar instruments.

Interviewing

Seidman (1998) stated that interviewing is the most suitable data collection method if we are to understand the experiences of others and the meanings they make of them. Interviews enable the researcher to learn the complexities of a participant's experiences from his or her own point of view. Following the advice of Mishler (1986), the best interviews are flexible and open ended, allowing for natural conversation. The goal is to understand each participant's experiences and perceptions related to a given situation in a nonthreatening way such that "meanings emerge, develop, and are shaped by and in turn shape the discourse."

Interviews are often audio recorded and subsequently transcribed. Transcription, however, can be laborious and time-consuming. You do not have the time needed to analyze data in such ways. Still, interviewing is a common and invaluable source of data for you.

Here are some guidelines to follow when using the interview technique for data collection:

1. Decide why you want to interview someone and what type of information you hope to glean from the interview.

2. Understand the difference between a structured interview and an informal one. A structured interview is one in which the interviewer has a high degree of control over the interview situation. A structured interview has an interview protocol that consists of a predetermined set of questions used by an interviewer. In contrast, an informal interview may occur without such a predetermined set of criteria or questions, but rather may be conducted informally, even casually, when speaking with someone. For those of you lacking interview experience, I recommend a structured format. As you develop confidence and skills, a more informal approach may be used.

3. Avoid the following:
   - Interrupting the participant
   - Failing to pick up on a topic that the participant considers important
   - Making inappropriate comments or jokes
   - Asking irrelevant personal questions (e.g., "How many children do you have?" unless it comes up in the normal course of "small talk")
   - Failing to check the tape recorder
   - Asking leading questions, such as "Don't you agree that principals should welcome teacher advice?"
   - Asking multiple questions, such as "Why was the supervisor union against shared decision making, and what do you think about the superintendent who was against merit pay?"
   - Inferring something not said or meant by the participant

4. Tips: Practice an actual interview with a friend, spouse, relative, or colleague; bring a tape recorder and extra blank tapes; organize your questions in advance; have fun; be a good listener; paraphrase the participant's main points; build rapport, especially at the beginning; probe when necessary; use a small, inconspicuous tape recorder, because a big one might make the participant self-conscious and consequently uncomfortable; ask questions when you do not understand what the participant meant; include open-ended questions such as "Take me through your day" or "Describe that meeting with the student"; and send out thank you cards or letters as soon as you complete interviews.

Tests

Tests are perhaps the most common tools used to collect data. Two typical tests are commonly used in data collection:

1. Criterion-referenced tests are one of two major types of testing instruments; these measure minimum levels of student performance. Teacher-made tests are one example of a criterion-referenced test. The teacher usually establishes an objective (or criterion) and then measures the extent to which students meet the objective. Criterion-referenced tests are one of many possible data collection sources.

2. Norm-referenced tests (synonymous with standardized tests) are one of two major types of testing instruments; these measure differences among individuals being tested. Each student's score is compared to the *norm* group, usually a nationally determined norm. A norm-referenced test, such as a standardized math test, can indicate how a given student, say 10-year-old Jerry, measures up against other 10-year-olds in the nation. For instance, if Jerry scores in the 65th percentile, this indicates that his score on the test was higher than 65% of 10-year-olds who took the test. Obviously, it also means that 35% scored higher than Jerry. Thus, norm-referenced tests compare students to other students on some preestablished norm or standard. Norm-referenced tests are usually used as important data collection sources.

Another data collection instrument (or data source) that is a kind of standardized or norm-referenced test is an achievement test. Achievement tests are commonly used measures or assessment tools in action research. An achievement test assesses an individual's knowledge or proficiency in a given content area. The Stanford Achievement Test and the Iowa Test of Basic Skills are examples of standardized achievement tests.

An achievement test is one form of data collection that may be used by an educational leader, for instance, to arrive at a decision about levels of student achievement in a particular content area. Analysis of results of these achievement tests may yield valuable information in terms of needed remediation in specific content areas.

Unfortunately, achievement or standardized tests are sometimes overused by supervisors and teachers who consider them the most important pieces of data when trying to arrive at a decision about levels of pupil achievement. Although an invaluable source of information, achievement tests should be considered as part of a portfolio of other assessment tools. No single assessment device should be used in making a decision about a program or practice. This book advocates a multidimensional, triangular approach to data collection.

Another data collection instrument that is a kind of standardized or norm-referenced test is an aptitude test. This test is designed to predict someone's ability to perform. The use of IQ tests is an example of an aptitude test. The Scholastic Aptitude Test (SAT) taken by precollegiate students is another example of an aptitude test.

School profile sheets may contain many of these aforementioned test scores. School profile sheets frequently analyze test scores over an extended period of time for various groups of students in different grades. As such, they are an invaluable source of information for you.

Useful information may also be gleaned from tests that do not provide quantitative outcomes. Writing samples, for instance, are usually marked holistically and can be used as qualitative data. Although no longer as common as they used to be, oral examinations may be yet another kind of test used to collect data.

Focus Groups

Focus groups (Krueger, 2000; Vaughn, Schumm, & Sinagub, 1996) are groups of individuals who are selected and consent voluntarily to share their views and opinions on specific topics. As a type of survey, a focus group is not unlike a group interview.

For example, as a principal in an elementary school, you may ask your upper-grade teachers to join you for a focused group session during lunchtime, during which you hear their opinions about the new textbook series adopted the previous year. Hearing their varied views may provide an invaluable method of data collection that may help your textbook committee arrive at a decision about continuing or discontinuing the series.

Secondary Data Collection Techniques

School Profile Data

School profile data sheets, generally available through the district office or state agencies (note that these may be called something different in your school or district), provide a wealth of important documentary information. These sheets provide reliable, clear data about a school's resources and students' needs in order to plan effectively for school improvement. These sheets provide achievement and background data over a period of years. Assessing student achievement over a four-year period, for example, is relatively easy. Data may include standardized reading and math scores by grade level over a four-year period; a statistical overview of a school's characteristics (percentage utilization, capacity, staff-student ratio, repair orders, etc.); demographic backgrounds of faculty, staff, and students; teacher characteristics (e.g., certification or tenure status); student characteristics (including mobility, class size, attendance rates).

Data derived from such profile sheets are easily obtained and interpreted. Such information may prove invaluable for collecting data about a specific program, practice, or procedure. Have you examined your school's profile sheet lately?

Multimedia

Too often, we neglect this valuable source for collecting data. Use of multimedia (including audiotape recordings, videotapes, films, photographs, and e-mail surveys, among others) has many advantages over more traditional methods for collecting data. Don't overlook using any of these media when collecting data.

For example, taking pictures of students showing how they feel about their projects is a wonderful, qualitative way of communicating information. Pictures *are* worth a thousand words. Pictures that show a group of eager, enthusiastic, and smiling kindergarten students holding their "Big Books" indicate the pride they must have felt in creating them. Using videotapes to film students' reading skills in September and videotaping them again in June will provide striking qualitative evidence of reading growth.

Although many researchers may indicate that use of videotape and photography may reflect a subjective bias, these forms of media, if incorporated properly and judiciously, can provide unique evidence. As long as you triangulate, that is, incorporate other valid and reliable data collection methods, multimedia use makes sense.

Portfolios

Portfolios are data collection instruments that include a great deal of information about a particular individual or group of individuals. Portfolios may include a student's achievement test scores, book reports, homework assignments, art projects, in-class tests, oral presentations, self-assessments, artwork, and so forth. Portfolios are excellent ways of collecting data from a variety of perspectives. Portfolios may later be analyzed qualitatively to arrive at a decision about the achievement levels, for example, of a particular student in language arts.

Records

School records, other than formal test data found in school profile sheets, are commonly referred to by educational leaders. You, for example, may collect data by examining cumulative record cards (revealing information about students); teacher files (revealing professional data about teachers, such as record of service); anecdotal records; and diaries, journals, or logs.

Reflective Question

1. How might you use each of the data collection instruments explained above to inform your decision making?

---

4. EASY STEPS TO PROGRAM EVALUATION

We as principals are often engaged in making decisions about various programs that either exist in our school already or ones under consideration for implementation. As such, we need to collect data to make decisions about the quality of these programs. You employ best practice in this effort by following these "easy steps" for program evaluation.

Program Evaluation in Five Steps

The discussion that follows is based on information gleaned from Sanders (2000).

The program I evaluated when I was a school administrator was first established at a public elementary school to address some of the needs of at-risk students. What made this program noteworthy was that martial arts training was incorporated as part of an overall curricular approach aimed at assisting selected fourth and fifth graders who were either currently involved in gangs or likely to join them. Program evaluation involved the following five steps.

I. Focusing the evaluation is composed of three steps:

1. Clarify evaluation purposes.

2. Clarify what is to be evaluated.

3. Identify questions to be answered.

In other words, in focusing our evaluation of the martial arts program, I attended to three aspects: clarifying the evaluation purposes, clarifying what was to be evaluated, and identifying the evaluation questions to be answered.

The purposes of our evaluation of the martial arts program were twofold:

1. To monitor pupil progress academically and socially—The intent was to conduct formative (in-progress) evaluations of the students' academic and social progress.

2. To monitor pupil motivation—The intent was to provide insights about the effort and persistence among student participants.

Our primary purpose for evaluating the program was to determine whether or not a program of this nature, which had never been attempted in our school before, should be continued and expanded to include other students at risk. Formative evaluative steps would enable us to monitor the program on an ongoing basis. Midcourse corrections could be made if necessary to improve the quality of the program. A summative evaluation was planned at the end of the school year by accumulating overall data relating to our two purposes outlined above as well as bringing in an outside consultant to provide his reactions to the program. The consultant was a principal of a school in another district who was also a black-belt instructor in the martial arts.

After clarifying evaluation purposes, another set of decisions was needed to get a clear sense of what, specifically, was to be evaluated. Specific criteria were specified separately for each of the evaluation purposes noted above. Five specific aspects were identified for pupil academic and social progress:

1. Incidence of aggressive behavior (physical fights with other students or physical acts toward faculty and staff)

2. Degree to which basic school and class rules were adhered to

3. Rates for tardiness and attendance

4. Number of homework assignments completed

5. Number of in-class assignments completed

Two specific aspects were identified for pupil motivation:

1. Degree to which students demonstrated effort and persistence in class

2. Degree to which students demonstrated effort and persistence in martial arts class

Once we had a sense of what was to be evaluated, evaluation questions were posed:

A. What were the expected academic outcomes for students who participated in the martial arts program?

B. What were the expected social outcomes for students who participated in the martial arts program?

C. Were students motivated to participate in in-class and school-related functions as well as in the martial arts class itself?

D. How well were the students performing on the expected outcomes noted above?

E. To what extent was the program meeting expectations of principal, assistant principal, martial arts instructor, teachers, parents, and student participants?

II. Collecting Data

In order to answer each of the evaluation questions, sources of information and evaluation methods for each evaluation question had to be identified. Scheduling the collection of data and assigning responsibility for collecting data were also attended to.

For data collection, information was culled from existing resources such as school files and records, direct observation of the program, and people in any way connected to the program. Evaluation methods that were deemed appropriate and feasible were matched to each evaluation question as follows:

A. What were the expected academic outcomes for students who participated in the martial arts program?

> *Data collection methods:* teacher and pupil interviews, teacher-made tests, and checklists for completed assignments.

B. What were the expected social outcomes for students who participated in the martial arts program?

> *Data collection methods:* teacher, supervisor, and pupil interviews; number of reported suspensions; number of times students were reported to assistant principal's office for misbehavior; attendance reports; and observations.

C. Were students motivated to participate in in-class and school-related functions as well as in the martial arts class itself?

> *Data collection methods:* teacher, supervisor, and pupil interviews; attendance reports; observations; student journals and portfolios; and visual anthropology or film ethnography (Marshall & Rossman, 1999).

D. How well were the students performing on the expected outcomes noted above?

> *Data collection methods:* methods noted above, through formative and summative evaluations.

E. To what extent was the program meeting expectations of principal, assistant principal, martial arts instructor, teachers, parents, and student participants?

> *Data collection methods:* interviews and questionnaires.

III. Organizing and Analyzing the Data

Evaluation methods provided much qualitative information. A large amount of data was gathered, especially through the use of multiple observers, multiple data collection methods, and extensive descriptions. Field notes; thick descriptions; transcripts of interviews; written responses to questionnaires; student journal entries; and copies of written documents, files, and reports were organized and analyzed according to each evaluation question. My concern was to summarize the data collected as accurately and clearly as possible. At every opportunity, I attempted to verify and validate the findings by getting reactions from people involved in the project.

IV. Reporting the Data

Results of this program evaluation revealed that the students at risk who participated in this integrated school curricular martial arts program improved in the following ways:

A. Academically—Although teachers initially reported little, if any, change in the numbers of completed homework and in-class assignments, by the end of the sixth month of the program teachers did in fact state that these assignments were increasingly being completed. Teachers who were interviewed stated that they were pleased by this academic progress. Teachers attributed this success not necessarily to the martial arts program per se, but to the close contact with and supervision of these students by supervisors and the martial arts instructor. In fact, the martial arts program did provide an incentive for these students to improve academically.

B. Socially—Teachers and supervisors reported fewer incidents of aggressive behavior exhibited by these students. A reduction in the number of discipline referrals was clearly evident. Classroom teachers also reported greater adherence to rules and procedures, as did teachers on lunch duty. Improved attendance and tardiness rates were noted.

C. Motivation—Classroom teachers and the martial arts instructor related that these students demonstrated greater effort, interest, and enthusiasm.

D. Expectations—Results from interviews, questionnaires, and informal observations and talks with parents, teachers, supervisors, and students themselves revealed positive feelings about the curricular martial arts program. Teachers and parents, in particular, asserted that they expected students to continue to improve.

Throughout the course of the evaluation, adult participants were informed about the evaluation process and the progress being made toward its completion. Time was spent obtaining comments from teachers, supervisors, and an outside consultant regarding any possible errors or omissions of evidence and other plausible interpretations that were missing. It was decided that the publication of an article describing our program could enhance efforts to expand the martial arts program to possibly include a larger sample and even expand the program to other schools. Reports of this evaluation, then, were to be disseminated throughout the district.

V. Administering the Evaluation

Administering this evaluation plan was a complex and arduous undertaking. Many logistics had to be considered, including scheduling data collection, allocating time for data analysis, and budget. Although budget constraints were minimal, scheduling problems emerged fairly regularly. At times, certain teachers, because of their own pressures and concerns, did not readily provide needed data. Programs had to be occasionally adjusted and arrangements coordinated with participants. Establishing and maintaining open communications among all participants were priorities. Anonymity of participants was ensured.

In sum, in order to assess the effectiveness of our martial arts program, I attended to five basic tasks in program evaluation (Sanders, 2000; also see Wholey, Hatry, & Newcomer, 1994): focusing the evaluation, collecting data, organizing and analyzing the data, reporting data, and administering the evaluation.

Summary

Five Steps in Planning an Evaluation

Focus the Evaluation

Collect Data

Organize and Analyze Data

Report the Data

Administer the Evaluation

Reflective Question

1. How might you use the information in this section of the chapter to make some decisions about key programs in your school that might affect the strategic initiatives in operation?

CONCLUSION

As a conclusion to this chapter, consider the following key questions that may serve as a guide to data-driven decision making in your school:

1. How might you encourage teachers to use data?

2. How can you build reflection into the school day, for you and teachers?

3. Why are students not learning?

4. What tools or strategies can you employ to discover patterns of student behavior and achievement in your school?

5. What might you need to collect such data?

6. Who will assist you in the process of data collection, analysis, and interpretation?

7. Who will draw conclusions and then take action?

8. What strategies can you employ to better promote student achievement?

9. How can you best foster a culture of improvement in your school?

10. Why is developing a learning community so important in order to promote data-based decision making?

"Leadership requires hard data and information for assessing growth and it also requires soft hearts and great spirit for successful, committed relationships, and courageous and intuitive decisions in the face of terrific challenges."

—Philip A. Streifer

CHAPTER FOUR

Best Practices in Transformational Leadership

"Leadership is one of the most observed and least understood phenomena on earth."

—James MacGregor Burns

"Rather than being a model that tells leaders what to do, transformational leadership provides a broad set of generalizations of what is typical of leaders who are transforming contexts."

—Peter G. Northouse

"To exercise leadership in this climate of change will require deep convictions, strong commitments, and clear ideas about directions for changes in the form and content of schooling."

—Robert J. Starratt

Leadership takes many forms. There have been almost as many leadership theories or approaches as there have been diet regimens. One of the more popular and well-researched forms of leadership is known as *transformational leadership*. Arising based on research in the 1980s, transformational leadership is aligned with attempts to change or transform individuals and the educational landscape as a whole. It combines both visionary and charismatic leadership approaches.

According to Northouse (2003), the term was first coined by Downton (1973, as cited by Northouse, 2003, p. 131). Yet it is acknowledged widely that James MacGregor Burns (1978), quoted above, amplified this approach to leadership in a landmark book titled, simply, *Leadership*. Burns, according to Northouse, identifies two types of leadership: transactional and transformational. The former represents the everyday interactions between manager and follower. Offering an incentive, for instance, to a follower for procedural compliance involves transactional leadership. In contrast, transformational leadership "refers to the process whereby an individual engages with others and creates a connection that raises the level of motivation and morality in both the leader and the follower" (Northouse, 2003, p. 131). Northouse provides an example of such a leader, drawn from the work of Burns: "Mahatma Gandhi as a classic example of transformational leadership . . . raised the hopes and demands of millions of his people and in the process was hanged himself" (p. 131). In this sense, transformational leadership is very much connected to visionary leadership, wherein the leader identifies a course of action based on a view or image of the future.

Another version of transformational leadership emerged with the work of House (1976), interestingly around the same time that Burns (1978) published his work. House's leadership construct focused on a personality trait of a leader known as *charisma*. Basing his work on Weber's (1947) classic theoretical model, House "suggested that charismatic leaders act in unique ways that have specific charismatic effects on their followers" (Northouse, 2003, p. 132). Charismatic, transformational leaders possess personal characteristics that include "being dominant, having a strong desire to influence others, being self-confident, and having a strong sense of one's own moral values" (p. 132). House's charismatic theory highlights four types of leadership behavior: such leaders serve as dynamic role models to foster their vision; they appear competent to others, especially their followers; they espouse points of view that have strong moral implications; and they communicate high expectations for performance. As a consequence of such leadership, several effects that are a direct result of charismatic leadership include the following:

follower trust in the leader's ideology, similarity between the follower's beliefs and the leader's beliefs, unquestioning acceptance of the leader, expression of warmth toward the leader, follower obedience, identification with the leader, emotional involvement in the leader's goals, heightened goals for followers, and follower confidence in goal achievement. Consistent with Weber, House contends that these charismatic effects are more likely to occur in contexts in which followers feel distress, because in stressful situations followers look to leaders to deliver them from their difficulties. (Northouse, 2003, p. 133)

A more recent version of transformational leadership emerged in the work of Bass (1985). Bass extended House's (1976) work by placing greater emphasis on the needs of followers rather than the leader and arguing that charisma by itself doesn't encapsulate all there is to know about transformational leadership. His model also more explicitly addresses how transformational leaders go about their work. He describes four kinds of influences such leaders utilize:

1. *Idealized influence*—refers to qualities a leader possesses to persuade or inspire others to action. Such leaders possess a charismatic quality that attracts followers. These followers depend on the leader's vision and high moral standing. Charismatic leaders can transform a system by rallying others around their vision by convincing followers of the necessity of the work that needs to be done.

2. *Inspirational motivation*—refers to the use of emotional appeals to encourage involvement in the ideal vision or ultimate goal. Inspirational leaders are articulate and encourage others through their words and deeds (e.g., through the use of symbolic leadership).

3. *Intellectual stimulation*—encourages followers to take responsibility for their actions. Such leaders encourage reflection and value input. Follower involvement is critical and is usually accomplished through problem-solving activities and projects.

4. *Individualized consideration*—demonstrates empathy and caring for the individual. Much time is spent nurturing, supporting, speaking with others, advising, coaching, and mentoring others.

According to Northouse (2003), "Transformational leadership helps followers to transcend their own self-interests for the good of the group or organization" (p. 137). Transformational leadership doesn't provide a recipe for leading but rather a way of thinking that emphasizes certain principles, as noted above.

The work of Bennis and Nanus (1985) also addressed transformational leadership. As a result of their extensive research into transformational leadership, four common approaches used by such leaders to accomplish their objectives have been identified:

> *"Treat others as you want to be treated yourself. If people are going to work for you and believe in what you are trying to accomplish for an organization, they will expect you to respect their interests and their views . . . a leader must recognize that his or her success depends upon the success of those who are being led."*
>
> —Gregory Anrig

1. Transformational leaders are visionaries. Although visions emerge from the leader, they are supported and reinforced by others. Leaders cannot be successful if others do not buy in to their vision.

2. Transformational leaders are social architects. They know how to work with people and groups of people. They navigate the organization with aplomb and are familiar with the politics of their job.

3. Transformational leaders engender trust and confidence. They are transparent in a positive sense. They are predictable and can be relied upon.

4. Transformational leaders possess self-regard. They know their strengths and weaknesses, and they can accentuate their positive qualities.

Summarizing how transformational leadership works, Northouse (2003) explains: "Transformational leaders set out to empower followers and nurture them in change. They attempt to raise the consciousness in individuals and to get them to transcend their own self-interests for the sake of others" (p. 142). Northouse highlights the following characteristics of transformational leaders: They serve as strong role models; have a highly developed sense of moral values; have a self-determined sense of identity; are visionary, confident, and articulate; have willingness to listen to followers; engender trust in followers; and act as change agents within and for the organization.

Although no theory of leadership is without criticisms (Northouse, 2003, pp. 144–146), transformational leadership informs our work as strategic leaders, because the purpose of strategizing is, in fact, meant to transform the school organization into a more conducive environment that promotes high achievement for all students.

This chapter suggests that strategic leaders are, in fact, involved in transformational leadership. Strategic leaders possess vision, look to the future, and build hope for student success. As such, they transform taken-for-granted notions of accepted practice. More practically, transformational leaders are astute politicians. They realize the influence of politics in their work and know that building political alliances is necessary to transform schools. Moreover, they see change as positive and necessary. In fact, they serve as change agents or facilitators of change in order to actualize their vision for the future of their school. They are leaders of change as they transform the school organization. This chapter discusses these ideas briefly and then suggests ways of enhancing your role as principal transformational leader.

What You Should Know About Transformational Leadership

- **Understanding Micropolitical Leadership**—The political insights of Duffy (2003), Bolman and Deal (1997), and Ramsey (2003) are highlighted.
- **Understanding, Planning, and Implementing Change**—Robbins and Alvy's (2003) suggestions are summarized.
- **Monitoring Change**—Horsley and Loucks-Horsley's (1998) CBAM process is highlighted.
- **Leading Change**—Kaser and colleagues' (2002) actions for effective leadership are highlighted.
- **Becoming a Transformational Leader**—We review Marazza's (2003) five essentials of organizational excellence that can help transform your school.

---

1. UNDERSTANDING MICROPOLITICAL LEADERSHIP

"Effective leadership in organizations results from the skillful interplay of power, politics, and ethics."

—Francis M. Duffy

"Today's principals find themselves within a highly charged environment amid social, economic, political, and cultural changes."

—William A. Owings and Leslie S. Kaplan

"Organizations are both arenas for internal politics and political agents with their own agendas, resources, and strategies."

—Lee G. Bolman and Terrence E. Deal

The expression "it's all politics" may not be entirely accurate, but at the same time, it isn't far off. Politics involving the vested interests of various individuals and groups of people within organizations plays a key role in shaping behavior and in what is or isn't accomplished in a school building. Various individuals and groups are vested with formal or even informal sources of power and authority. As principal, for instance, you are vested by the nature of your status or position with a degree of authority over, for example, tenure decisions over faculty. *Power* is a term that refers to the extent to which we use the authority vested in us. You may, for instance, have the authority to dock the pay of an individual who commits some indiscretion, but it doesn't mean you have to exercise your power to do so. Quite often, principals do not invoke their authority to do such things. Although formal authority may exist in different individuals within a school (e.g., financial school secretary, custodian, first-grade lead teacher, and assistant principal), informal authority or the authority to act powerfully might rest with charismatic leaders, for instance. Maria Rodriguez, a 12th-grade science teacher, may not occupy a formal position of authority in the school, but given her charismatic nature, other teachers and staff look up to her because she is a staunch, articulate advocate for teacher and student rights in the school.

The study of politics is at once complicated and necessary in order for us to navigate the educational landscape in a school. Although this is not necessarily the place to delve into the intricacies of such a discussion, its mention is significant given our discussion of principal strategic leadership. Planning and making decisions, important parts of strategic leadership, do not occur in isolation from the political realities or exigencies that exist in schools. Attending to issues of vested interests, authority, and power within schools is necessary to carry out our strategic initiatives. In the example that follows, Mr. Martucci cannot carry out his strategic initiative without mindful attention to the political landscape in his school:

> *"The principal of a renewing school, usually its most visible public figure, can become a lightning rod for controversy and disparaging remarks."*
>
> —Carl D. Glickman

Mr. Martucci, a high school principal, is newly appointed to Ridgefield High in a suburban section of Illinois. The former principal was removed by the superintendent for "incompetence." Further explanation reveals that the former principal did not get along with most faculty members, he ostracized parents, and student achievement scores in most areas were on a steady decline over a five-year period. Mr. Martucci is also entering a school with low teacher morale, because the former principal, according to the superintendent, "played favorites among faculty and staff . . . and was anti-union." "He always stretched the truth to suit his position," explained one union representative. "He continually bent the rules to accomplish his agenda; that is, more power for himself and his cronies." Mr. Martucci understands this background and wishes to utilize his skills as a collaborative and strategic school leader to break through what he perceives as "schoolwide complacency and general malaise." He wants to rally faculty and staff around a new vision of excellence but one couched within an atmosphere of social justice and equity for all. He realizes the school needs a collaboratively developed and monitored strategic plan. He intends to undertake a careful and patient needs assessment to better under-stand the school and its "players." He wants to foster good interpersonal rela-tionships, which are so critical to nurturing a sound and effective political environment. Good interrelations, however, is not enough, he knows. He needs to carefully examine and consider these questions, among others:

1. What are the vested interests in this school?
2. Who are the key political players?
3. Who makes various decisions?
4. How can the vested interests of one group coincide favorably with such interests of another group?
5. What role can various people or groups play in the overall strate-gic plan initiative?
6. How can conflicts be minimized or managed?
7. Will I, as principal, have the support I need from the superinten-dent and other district officials?

Duffy (2003) posits that power and politics are expected processes that occur naturally in school settings. As such, Duffy continues, they are "neutral." He explains, "There is nothing inherently wrong or evil with power and politics . . . the exercise of power and politics must, I believe, be done in an ethical manner" (p. 15).

The relationship among power, politics, and ethical behavior is stressed by Duffy (1991), as depicted in Figure 4.1.

Examining the figure, you'll notice that four quadrants are formed by the intersecting lines. Each quadrant represents a different sort of

Figure 4.1   Relationship Among Power, Politics, and Ethical Behavior

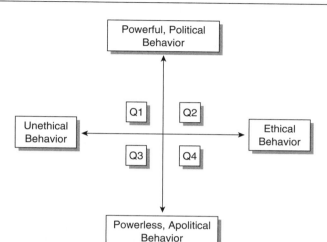

leader behavior. Quadrant 1 (Q1) represents a leader who displays powerful, political behavior in an unethical manner. Quadrant 2 (Q2) reflects a powerful, political, and ethical leader. Quadrant 3 (Q3) represents an unethical leader who is powerless and apolitical. Quadrant 4 (Q4) indicates that the leader may display ethical behavior but is powerless and apolitical. Principal behavior can be characterized in each quadrant as follows:

- Q1: Powerful, political, but unethical behaviors
  Reflective Activity: Can you provide a case example? Describe in detail.

- Q2: Powerful, political, and ethical behaviors
  Reflective Activity: Can you provide a case example? Describe in detail.

- Q3: Powerless, apolitical, and unethical behaviors
  Reflective Activity: Can you provide a case example? Describe in detail.

- Q4: Powerless, apolitical, but ethical behaviors
  Reflective Activity: Can you provide a case example? Describe in detail.

Duffy (1991) explains that Quadrant 2 behavior represents best practice. Leaders who inspire through vision building, who have the ability to "work the system" to get things accomplished, to create structures and systems that allow for wide participation and collaboration, to obtain and utilize resources legitimately, to motivate followers to good and meaningful action, and to do the right and moral things fit nicely into Q2. Duffy (2003), advocating Q2 leadership, explains why some leaders cannot lead in this way and then raises a critical question that, although it may go beyond our analysis here, is still important:

> In my heart I know most people who move into leadership positions want to be Q2 leaders. But something happens to them when they actually make the move to the administrator's office. Somehow some of them lose their sense of moral direction, their notions of rightness and wrongness, their definitions of truth and justice, and they frequently seek expedient solutions to problems without regard to underlying ethical principles. Then, before long, they change into Q1s, Q3s, or Q4s. This presents a management development problem for school districts: how do they recruit leaders who are capable of and willing to be Q2 leaders, and how do they restructure their district's reward system to help leaders stay within the Q2 arena? The solution to this puzzle is, I believe, important to the future of leadership for systematic school improvement. (pp. 18–19)

Bolman and Deal (1997) have written much in the area of political leadership. They summarize "five propositions" using their perspective as follows (p. 163):

1. Organizations are *coalitions* of various individuals and interest groups.

2. There are *enduring differences* among coalition members in virtues, beliefs, information, interests, and perceptions of reality.

3. Most important decisions involve the allocation of *scarce resources*—who gets what.

4. Scarce resources and enduring differences give *conflict* a central role in organizational dynamics and make *power* the most important resource.

5. Goals and decisions emerge from *bargaining, negotiation,* and *jockeying for position* among different stakeholders.

Each of their propositions finds relevance in our discussion of strategic leadership. Putting forth and maintaining a strategic vision requires the participation of others, as we mentioned earlier. Building and nurturing coalitions of support is critical to your success as strategic leader. Discovering who has a vested interest in your vision of the future and capitalizing on ways to involve them are essential. Although you strive to build coalitions, you realize fully that they comprise diverse community members with different perspectives and capabilities. You cherish such diversity, because you realize that the strategic plan will be made even stronger through diversity of ideas and points of view. You are a pragmatist as well. You know that resources are scarce, and so prioritization is necessary. Keeping channels of communication open by sharing your views and priorities is a way to build and maintain support for your initiatives. You know that conflicts will arise, but you are prepared. You are prepared to bargain, negotiate, and jockey for position without infringing on others' rights and perspectives. You aim to achieve consensus, if possible, in most matters.

On a more practical level, Ramsey (2003) provides tips on handling politics that are relevant to your work every day. Below are some of Ramsey's shrewd suggestions for navigating the political environment (pp. 113–114):

1. Understand the organization. Who has the power? Why? How did they get it? And how do they use it?

2. Never underestimate the other guy (especially an opponent). Don't assume anything about anyone.

3. Develop alliances on all levels.

4. Learn how to schmooze.

5. The best political move is always to make the boss(es) look good.

6. Invite your enemies into your inner circle. That way, you know what they are doing.

7. Try not to burn bridges or sever any relationships permanently.

8. Try to stay out of petty internal politics.

Reflective Question

1. How do Bolman and Deal's (1997) "wellsprings of power" (see the following list) inform your work as strategic leader? Provide examples.

Bolman and Deal (1997, pp. 169–170) describe the following eight sources of power:

1. *Position power (authority).* Positions confer certain levels of formal authority—professors assign grades, and judges decide disputes. Positions also place incumbents in more or less powerful locations in communications and power networks. It helps to be in the right unit as well as the right job: a lofty title in a backwater department may not mean much, but junior members of a powerful unit may have substantial clout.

2. *Information and expertise.* Power flows to those who have information and know-how to solve important problems. . . .

3. *Control of rewards.* The ability to deliver jobs, money, political support, or other rewards brings power. . . .

4. *Coercive power.* Coercive power rests on the ability to constrain, block, interfere, or punish. A union's ability to walk out, students' ability to sit in, and an army's ability to clamp down all exemplify coercive power.

5. *Alliances and networks.* Getting things done in organizations involves working through a complex network of individuals and groups. Friends and allies make that a lot easier. . . .

6. *Access and control of agendas.* A by-product of networks and alliances is access to decision arenas. Organizations and political systems typically give some groups more access than others. When decisions are made, the interests of those with "a seat at the table" are well represented, while the concerns of absentees are often distorted or ignored.

7. *Framing: control of meaning and symbols.* "Establishing the framework within which issues will be viewed and decided is often tantamount to determining the result." Elites and opinion leaders often have substantial ability to define and even impose the meanings and myths that define identify, beliefs, and values. Viewed positively, this provides meaning and hope. Viewed cynically, elites can convince others to accept and support things not in their best interests. This can be a very subtle and unobtrusive form of power: when the powerless accept the myths promulgated by the powerful, overt conflict and power struggles may disappear.

8. *Personal power.* Individuals with charisma, energy and stamina . . . are imbued with power independent of other sources.

2. UNDERSTANDING, PLANNING, AND IMPLEMENTING CHANGE

Robbins and Alvy (2003) address some fundamental ideas about the change process, so integral to transformational leadership, that represent best practice, especially during the initial stages of the process. Below, I review some of their ideas:

- "Change brings loss and resistance" (p. 69)—I challenge my students to cross their hands over their chest. Then I say, "Reverse your arms now." Many of them naturally hesitate a bit. Change is not easy. We are often set in our ways, our habits. Organizations are no different. Change, explain Robbins and Alvy, may encourage a sense of feeling of "loss and insecurity." Consequently, people may resist efforts to change. You should understand these natural feelings whenever you introduce any significant change. Curiously, though, from my experience, these precise feelings of loss and resistance might become the very means to lead the group to a better understanding of the change process and what is involved in the reform effort. This positive move can occur only if the leader is cognizant of how people may initially react to change.

- "Influencing individuals and the institution" (pp. 69–70)—As principal, you should remain sensitive to "individuals affected by change and the institution that is transformed as a result of change." Balancing the needs of the individual with organizational requirements has been a long-standing issue in the field of organizational change (Lunenburg & Ornstein, 2004). In this context, you should view the "organization" as comprising "individuals." That is, nothing long-lasting can occur without the willing participation of people.

- "Building trust for successful change" (pp. 70–71)—As principal, you play the most critical role in building trust among parties to change. If you "preach" collaboration, for instance, make certain your actions reflect such assertions. Empower others through decision-making committees, for example, to offer their input.

- "Conflict can contribute to positive change" (pp. 71–72)—Conflict is often avoided and seen as negative. Effective strategic leaders understand that conflict is inevitable in this process and that "conflicting ideas

> "[Leadership is] mobilizing people to tackle tough problems."
>
> —Ron Heifetz

should be welcomed as providing valuable sources of information and insight to assist in planning for change or enhancing a change effort once it has begun."

- "Strategies to promote trust" (pp. 72–73)—The authors explain that "because risk taking, experimentation, and voicing conflicting opinions are essential ingredients for change," a trusting environment must be established. They offer the following suggestions that are relevant to our work as principals:
  1. "Walk your talk."—As we mentioned earlier, let your actions reflect your words.
  2. "Lead by personal example."—For instance, don't encourage someone to do something if you are not prepared to act similarly.
  3. "Encourage people to talk about what it means to be trustworthy."—Spend time at formal and informal gatherings to discuss what it means to be trustworthy. Open communication and discussion are essential.
  4. "Invite staff members to have input into collectively determining what the change will be and how it will be implemented."—Collaborative leadership is essential.
  5. "Encourage consensus-building activities."—Encourage a win-win situation when it comes to decision making. Voting for proposals means there will be "losers."
  6. "Keep lines of communication open." They explain, "This helps to dispel rumors and encourages dialogue and healthy interaction to engender mutual support."
  7. "Encourage disagreement."—If you do not, people will keep their dissatisfactions to themselves, and these ill feelings may emerge at inappropriate or inopportune times.
  8. "Celebrate small and large successes."—Use positive reinforcements and encouragements along the way.

- "Assumptions about change" (pp. 73–74)—According to the authors, "Creating a culture of trust is a prerequisite to implementing change." However, according to Fullan and Stiegelbauer (1991, cited by Robbins & Alvy, 2003, p. 73), we must consider various assumptions about change that go along with such trust building:
  1. Your view of change represents only one perspective; seek other points of view.
  2. Whenever an idea emerges to change something, that idea may be interpreted differently by different stakeholders.

Assume, Robbins and Alvy say, "that any significant innovation, if it is to result in change, requires individual implementors to work out their own meaning."

3. Conflict, as alluded to earlier, is not only inevitable but critical to "successful change."
4. People need encouragement and support throughout the change process.
5. Change takes time. Deep change may take, from my experience, three to five years.
6. Problems with implementing change are inevitable. Don't assume that initial difficulties mean that folks are against the change. Inquire, communicate, nurture, and remain persistent.
7. Not everyone will rally, at least initially, around the idea for change.
8. Assume you need a well-developed plan to implement and sustain the change.
9. Change is a messy, nonlinear process.
10. "Assume that change is a frustrating, discouraging business."

• "Three phases of change" (pp. 74–75)—The mobilization phase is the first stage you must consider. A thorough needs assessment and gathering of relevant data are essential prior to implementing any major change. The implementation phase includes training and small scale tryout of the idea, if possible. The institutionalization phase occurs when the change is widely accepted by most stakeholders.

Bolman and Deal's (1997) comments serve as a fitting conclusion:

There is no guarantee that those who gain power will use it wisely or justly. But it is not inevitable that power and politics are demeaning and destructive. Constructive politics is a possibility—indeed, a necessary possibility if we are to create institutions and societies that are both just and efficient. (p. 175)

Reflective Question

1. What specific strategies could you utilize to practically implement each of the suggestions above?

3. MONITORING CHANGE

The change process is complex, to say the least. A key to successful change is monitoring its development from the very beginning. A popular approach for doing so is known as the Concerns-Based Adoption Model (CBAM; Horsley & Loucks-Horsley, 1998). Jack Newman is a new principal in a school in which teachers had not had previous experience in collaborative work because the former principal employed autocratic methods of administration. Jack, trained in CBAM, thought that this approach to dealing with change was ideal because it focused on individual needs and interests. Confiding in his superintendent, Jack said, "My teachers are suspicious of change and, consequently, of me. They are dedicated to their job but deep down I think they want a better school. I know my use of the CBAM will suit them perfectly."

The model considers above all else how the individual deals with the change process. Let's discuss the model as if Jack Newman were actually implementing it. The CBAM acknowledges that the individual may pass through seven stages related to dealing with change:

- Stage 0: Awareness—Teachers in Jack's school have little, if any, concern or involvement with change. In this case, Jack realizes it's not that they are against innovative practices, but many of them are rather ambivalent. They have this new principal and are now wondering if he will be anything like their former principal.

- Stage 1: Informational—Rumors spread about some of the new ideas Jack has to lead the school. People ask themselves, "What is this new change all about?" They want more information. They finally hear Jack talk about collaboration and teamwork to implement a new block-scheduling system in the school to allow for more continuous teaching time on literacy and mathematics. Many teachers are surprised to see Jack soliciting their advice and suggestions.

- Stage 2: Personal—Jack realizes that change, long-lasting change, requires individual commitment and interest. Keeping the needs of each teacher in mind, he knows teachers will ask themselves, "How will this change affect me? What will be my personal involvement? Will this create more work for me? What are the advantages and disadvantages? What more do I need to learn about this innovative idea?" Jack reaches out to teachers one on one and offers workshops by calling in experts on block scheduling and other topics. He takes a few teachers to a school that has implemented block scheduling successfully.

- Stage 3: Management—The previous two steps involved self-concerns. Jack's task is to allay apprehensions, invite input and partici-pation, and gain the confidence of at least a few teachers willing to try the new idea. Now, it's task or management time. Teachers will ask, "What do I need to do to make this innovation a reality in my class-room? How do I implement block scheduling? Who will assist me? What more needs to be done?"

- Stage 4: Consequence—Jack realizes that any innovative prac-tice will be measured not only by the impact it has on student learning (which of course is most important) but also by the degree to which teachers view this innovation as helpful and meaningful to their own work in the classroom. They may ask themselves, "Does this innovative idea help me accomplish my goals? Do I believe this new practice will make a difference? What impact will it have on student motivation to learn? Ultimately, will students learn better?"

- Stage 5: Collaboration—Although Jack knows that collaboration is essential at every stage when implementing change, he focuses on the initial stages of implementation by encouraging teacher-to-teacher dialogue. Teachers share their reactions and experiences with one another on shared preps. He encourages them to ask, "How will work-ing with my teaching partner help me better implement block schedul-ing? What can I learn from my colleagues about, for instance, dealing with disciplinary issues that arise as a result of increased class time? What can I learn from others about extended instructional time? What can I share with others that might benefit them?" Teachers realize that success depends on each of them working with others. Jack facilitates this important process.

- Stage 6: Refocusing—Jack knows change involves continuous focus on the innovative practice and an analysis of how teachers are dealing with it. He constantly refocuses by asking, "What else do teachers need to succeed? What additional support can I offer? How can I sustain interest over time? How will I deal with problems such as teacher resistance?"

These seven stages in the CBAM process are sequential, but the amount of time devoted to each varies greatly. In Jack's case, he knows he'll have to spend a great deal of time at the first three stages to build teacher interest and motivation, given their past experiences with the former principal. The major benefit from CBAM was that Jack, as strate-gic leader, was attentive to individual concerns. Word spread, and teachers realized that Jack was indeed different from their former principal. He showed that he cared about them by listening to their concerns. As one teacher commented, "He listens. He realized that I needed more time to accept this change. He worked with me." The advantage to the CBAM process, explains Jack, "is not about the innovation per se; rather, it's about how one goes about dealing with people. It's helping them accommodate to the change at their own pace. After all," Jack concludes, "without individual commitment, no innovation will last."

Jack shares his knowledge of the CBAM process with principal colleagues at a district workshop. He explains:

> The CBAM process focuses on the affective dimensions of change. In the seven stages of concern I previously explained above four general categories are evident: awareness, self, task, and impact. Beyond these stages of concern, CBAM also involves levels of use.

He continues, "Levels of use address the behavior dimensions each teacher may go through in making any change a reality in the classroom." Jack reviews these seven levels "that are so critical if change is to occur at the individual level."

- Level 0: Nonuse—Mrs. Johnson refuses to implement the change. She's not interested, unwilling, or fearful of change. Her teaching practice remains unchanged at this point.

- Level 1: Orientation—Mrs. Johnson hears others talk enthusiastically about the change. Still reluctant, she nevertheless gathers information by reading some literature distributed at a faculty conference.

- Level 2: Preparation—This third level took Mrs. Johnson a full year to reach. She now has decided to give block scheduling a try at the start of the new academic year. She is prepared to give it a shot.

- Level 3: Mechanical—Mrs. Johnson implements the innovation but doesn't feel comfortable. She says, "It's like when I was a beginning teacher, I was so nervous that I read from the manual as I was giving a lesson. I feel so inadequate." Jack explains that Mrs. Johnson is not giving up but simply articulating her discomfort at the newness of it all. "It's so important," he explains, "to provide teachers at this stage with the moral encouragement they need to see the innovation through."

- Level 4: Routine and refinement—As time passes, Mrs. Johnson feels more at ease. She likes the added time and no longer feels so rushed to complete a lesson. "I can offer more remedial assistance without having to leave many students behind as we progress through the curriculum unit." Her day now becomes more routine. She also begins to refine her teaching techniques to match the longer class periods. She differentiates instruction by using cooperative learning, which, she says, "takes so much time . . . that I now have!"

- Level 5: Integration—Mrs. Johnson at this stage is now willing to share her experiences with others and even joins a subcommittee to plan for additional professional development for teachers in the school.

- Level 6: Renewal—At this stage, Mrs. Johnson is ready and able to offer suggestions for refining the innovation. Perhaps, she might even extend the instructional practice or introduce a new yet related innovative practice. As she does so, she's aware of Levels of Concern and Levels of Use.

Continuing to explain the process, Jack says,

According to the early developers of CBAM, change must be viewed as a gradual process that occurs slowly and steadily over time. Change is not time related in that it occurs at a precise moment. Change is not an event; it's a process. Also essential is the notion that change is developmental and an intensely personal experience. As principals, we must be attentive to the needs of each teacher and not expect that all people will react to change in the same way or progress at the same pace. That's the advantage to CBAM. It encourages us to consider, most importantly, the needs, interests, and abilities of the individual in the change process.

Reflective Questions

1. How might you incorporate the CBAM approach? Be specific.

2. Find out more about the CBAM change process. It's a bit more complicated than described above. What else did you learn about it?

---

4. LEADING CHANGE

Kaser and colleagues (2002) highlight essential actions for effective leadership that warrant attention. The authors group their discussion about change around four themes:

1. Change works best as a process that is planned and guided.

As a process, change occurs over time and should not be conceived as a single event (e.g., changing an aspect of a program to include for purchasing 10 additional laptop computers). According to Kaser et al. (2002), leaders who view change as a single event will not include others in decision making and will manage from a hierarchical frame of reference. They say that leaders who conceive of change as a process do the following (p. 63):

- Involve the people affected by the change in planning for the change
- Know that any significant change takes time and plan accordingly
- Employ professional development over time to ensure that people acquire the right knowledge and skills to implement the change
- Set realistic expectations for implementation

Kaser et al. (2002) also emphasize that effective leaders plan for change by establishing a formal plan that includes a list of "desired outcomes"; "a guide for achieving" them; and "a means for others to monitor how well a change effort is progressing," one that ensures "alignment . . . between the vision, mission(s), goals, and activities," binds "different parts of the organization together," and "sets forth evaluation criteria" (p. 71).

Kaser et al. (2002) also emphasize that change must be viewed within a "continuous improvement" paradigm. That is, effective principals do not fear change but use it to improve their school. These leaders, of course, also realize that change is complex and often unpredictable. They say, "Change is a journey marked by detours, dead ends, and clover leafs, with an occasional stretch of clear motoring along the way" (p. 75).

2. Change occurs best when people who work within the organization change.

Change is a process that involves people planning, sharing, discussing, reacting, and problem solving. Change doesn't occur in a vacuum. Effective principal leaders always consider people's "personal satisfactions, frustrations, concerns, motivations, and perceptions" involving the change process (p. 78).

Because change is complicated and uneven, some people may not adapt to change as easily as others. Effective leaders realize this fact and remain sensitive to individual reactions. Open communication and active involvement every step of the way, as much as is possible, will do much to alleviate some people's apprehensions about change.

Changing people's views or beliefs is not easy. For instance, if you want your school to change to a more inclusive pedagogical and instructional orientation, then you must have teachers who are committed to such practice. Merely implementing inclusive practices without buy-in and professional development opportunities is doomed to failure. Change takes time, and sometimes not all people will come on board at the same time. Realize this fact, and work first with individuals who share your vision; over time, some others will join along.

> *"Outstanding schools have effective principals. Effective principals develop outstanding schools."*
>
> —James O'Hanlon and Donald O. Clifton

3. Principals must lead change.

Principals cannot expect that everyone will be equally motivated to join in on the change. Reviewing the work of Richard Barrett, Kaser et al. (2002) highlight four dimensions of motivation: physical, emotional, mental, and spiritual. They explain:

The physical and emotional dimensions are satisfied primarily by external conditions. For example, financial reward is an example of the physical component; open communication is an example of the emotional. Physical and emotional aspects can be fulfilled by either positive external incentives (e.g., promotions) or negative external incentives (e.g., loss of status). The efficiency of external rewards declines over time and so must be increased to remain motivational. (p. 89)

Leading change, according to Kaser et al. (2002), who rely here on the work of Peter Senge, involves "personal mastery." They explain: "There are three characteristics of personal mastery: a strong sense of personal vision, a commitment to learning to see reality more clearly, and the ability to clarify continually what is most important to us" (p. 95).

Another essential point the authors raise regarding leading change involves developing the skills necessary to tackle resistance to change. Three of their suggestions include the following (p. 103):

- Determine the concerns of the resisters. Respond with the appropriate intervention.
- Help resisters make the connection between their personal visions and the organizational vision.
- Set up a timetable that allows adequate assimilation time.

Kaser et al. (2002) conclude with a cautionary note:

> If the degree or extent of resistance seems greater than would normally be expected, leaders should look at the change initiative itself. Perhaps it is not the appropriate initiative for the time or circumstances. Maybe there is a better solution waiting. Knowing people's specific objections can help you determine if you need to reconsider what you are proposing. (p. 104)

4. Pay attention to organizational needs.

Kaser et al. (2002) accentuate the importance of systemic thinking, that is, looking for the root causes for organizational problems. A simple example of systemic thinking could involve finding solutions for why faculty do not collaborate with one another. As principal, you might ask: "What structural mechanisms have I established in terms of scheduling, for example, that may better facilitate increased faculty involvement or meeting times?" According to Kaser et al., systems thinking "is a particular way of looking at organizational behavior. It is a body of knowledge and tools that helps identify underlying patterns and suggests how they can be changed" (p. 118).

Organizations have their own character based on past events and current cultural norms and mores. Some organizations, for example, are more apt to accept change or reform than others. A school community, for instance, that has been administered by a bureaucratic tyrant for years may not have developed the collaborative skills and support mechanisms that are most conducive to community involvement. Another school, with a leader who is more collaborative in her approach, is more likely to remain receptive to community participation. Kaser et al. (2002) maintain that leaders of organizations can do much to help launch and sustain change initiatives. Here are some actions principals may take (p. 124):

- Involve the appropriate stakeholders.
- Think systemically.
- Cultivate a high level of urgency for change.
- Use data for decision making.

- Create structures with minimal hierarchy.
- Exhibit a high level of risk taking.
- Promote resiliency in people and the organization.
- Designate benchmarks and acknowledge achievement of the benchmarks.

Kaser et al. (2002) conclude: "Organizations today don't have the luxury [of] being able to reject or accept the opportunity to change. They must change, or they will cease to exist. The only open question is how successful they will be with whatever change initiatives they undertake" (p. 125).

Reflective Questions

1. To what extent do you lead for change? Give concrete examples or instances.

2. How do you "get" people to change?

3. What strategies above work best for you as a leader of change?

---

5. BECOMING A TRANSFORMATIONAL LEADER

The literature is replete with theories and strategies to achieve transformational leadership. Consult the selected works enumerated in the Best Resources section of this book. One of the more recent attempts to help practitioners transform their organizations is very concise and useful. Marazza's (2003) Five Essentials to achieve educational excellence is very relevant to our discussion of strategic leadership. Five Essentials include:

- Plan strategically—According to Marazza (2003), "Thinking and planning strategically begins with conversation" (p. 3). As principal, you are key here to encourage and facilitate productive conversations in formal and informal ways with teams of teachers, parents, administrators, and even, at times, students. Meaningful conversations are conducted around common problems, school challenges, and the ideas necessary to solve or alleviate them. Marazza offers the following useful suggestions, among others, to get this First Essential moving:

1. Identify a group leader or facilitator who has superior interpersonal skills and who is trusted and open minded.
2. The leader should encourage open conversation aimed at problem solving without anyone criticizing or disparaging an idea. The point here is to generate ideas to move the plan and group forward. Keep in mind not to rush in order to get the team moving. Soliciting and receiving views from all stakeholders and the discussion that ensues take time. Without this open conversation, all future initiatives might be jeopardized.
3. Ensure that each participant has a chance to participate in decision making, whether through consensus, vote, or some other system.

Marazza (2003) reminds us that "building principals must learn the skills of active engagement and mutual trust development." He adds this piece of advice for those involved in the whole strategic process: "Trust," he says, "must be generated in order for the conversations of those involved in the strategic process to be effective" (p. 4). The point here is that strategic planning is an essential component of transformational leadership, and for this process to be effective, trust among relevant parties must be ensured.

• Benchmark for excellence—Transforming schools involves setting priorities and measurable goals. Benchmarking, according to Marazza (2003), is an effective method to achieve "organizational success" in this way (p. 38). As principal, you need to establish some preexisting criteria to help guide your strategic plan. Marazza advises that we ask ourselves the degree to which we have the following items in place:

1. A system to measure school performance internally. For instance, if one of your major academic areas needs improvement (e.g., math scores among fifth graders), you may want to compare fifth-grade performances over the past several years. Such comparisons will give the committee a better basis of comparisons to determine the degree of student success or lack thereof.
2. A system to measure school performance externally. Comparing, for instance, fifth-grade scores in your school with those of other schools in the district or neighboring ones, especially fifth graders in schools with similar demographic patterns. These comparisons make for more accurate and fairer analyses.

3. A system to share school best practices across grade levels and school buildings.
4. An assessment system to compare results to external standards.
5. Use of benchmark data to initiate improvements—instructional, curricular, or otherwise.

• Lead collaboratively—According to Marazza (2003), "Collaboration is the means to establishing and sustaining a systematic effort that brings together all school stakeholders with the common interest of using their combined wisdom to both solve problems and advance school improvement initiatives using consensus decision making" (p. 9). Collaborative leadership is a necessary prerequisite for strategic leadership. Strategic planning does not occur in a vacuum. Collaborative leadership, according to Marazza (p. 46), demands

1. An open-minded attitude, receptive to new ideas
2. Respect for colleagues and their opinions
3. Thoughtful consideration of divergent ideas
4. A tolerance for ambiguity, which inevitably develops as you work your way through to new solutions
5. Professional ego strength (don't let a traditional "boss" ego or mentality rule your approach)
6. Open access for all to all information
7. Patience to listen to others as you work ideas through to a conclusion.

• Engage the public—Transforming schools cannot occur without engaging a broader constituency. Marazza (2003) encourages us to consider these questions:

1. Does the principal meet with parents and the public (i.e., other community members) on a regular basis?
2. Does the principal seek written feedback from parents on ways to involve them in school affairs?
3. Are the public and parents meaningfully involved in conversations regarding the future of the school?
4. Do professional staff members sincerely believe the public can assist the school?
5. Does the school have a systematic and regularly implemented process of involving parents in decision making about the curriculum?
6. Is the public familiar with the school's strategic plan initiatives?

7. Does the principal facilitate ongoing meetings between educators and the public?
8. Do parents believe the school will act on their input?
9. Does the public have a stake in school affairs and decisions?
10. Has the school formed positive working relations with the parents and public?

• Govern by standards.—School transformation is purposeful, measurable, and planned. Marazza (2003) provides these questions for our consideration:

1. Does the school have clearly written standards defining excellence?
2. Are these standards communicated to all stakeholders?
3. Does the school continuously hold meetings to ensure that progress is monitored?
4. Are assessments used to measure progress and make appropriate curricular changes to improve student achievement?
5. Does the public feel that the school's standards of excellence reflect "top" performance?
6. Is there an alignment between the school's standards of excellence and allocation of resources?
7. Do the standards of excellence reflect unambiguous and comprehensive goals?

Transformational leaders support change, as Marazza (2003) states: "In schools today, transformation comes from an environment that is supportive of change and innovation" (p. 69). Taken as a whole, the Five Essentials briefly reviewed above "empower the organizational stakeholders to work productively together to not only accomplish their organizational mission but also to achieve organizational performance excellence" (p. 129). Schools will not be able to enhance student learning and achievement unless a culture of change is accepted. As Marazza concludes (p. 147):

The promise of improved student learning opportunities is dependent upon the effective transformation of school organizations. Transforming organizations mixes many ingredients, none more important than people. Understanding relationships requires deep listening skills, none more important than person-to-person. Finally, designing school transformations enjoin[s] a confluence of people, conceptual understandings, and commitment to a commonly derived meaning of the organization. The Five Essentials provide the skills necessary to work our way though the challenge of organizational transformation.

Reflective Question

1. How might you use Marazza's Five Essentials in your work to transform your school?

CONCLUSION

Transforming schools is easy if done superficially. Such change, however, is ephemeral. Unfortunately, much change, says Fullan (2003b), occurs at this superficial level. In fact, he says, much of the change in schools in the 1960s around innovative instructional and curricular practices were short-lived because they were implemented on the surface without a deep change in people's beliefs and behavior. Both Fullan (2003b) and Starratt (1995) concur that change without effecting a change in core beliefs and values is doomed to remain temporary and superficial. "Transformational leadership," says Starratt, "is concerned with large, collective values" (p. 110). All the aforementioned best practices are predicated on the foundation of changing core beliefs and values. Fullan (1991, cited in Fullan, 2003b) has identified in *Leading in a Culture of Change*

> five crucial mind and action sets that leaders in the 21st century must cultivate: a deep sense of moral purpose, knowledge of the change process, capacity to develop relationships across diverse individuals and groups, skills in fostering knowledge creation and sharing, and the ability to engage with others in coherence making amidst multiple innovations. (p. 35)

Strategically minded principals want to transform their schools deeply, not artificially and superficially. Doing so takes time and effort within a collaborative and empowering paradigm. Our work in this area is fundamental and morally imperative. Such work, moreover, is necessary, because transformational leadership has been linked to student achievement. Cotton (2003), who has conducted one of the most extensive reviews of the literature in the field, states quite emphatically:

Not surprisingly, researchers find that transformational leadership is positively related to student achievement and is more effective than the deal-making between principal and staff that characterizes the transactional approach alone. (p. 61)

"The work of leadership involves attention to shared learning that leads to shared purpose and action."

—Linda Lambert

Conclusion

Making Strategic Leadership a Reality

This book has underscored the importance of planning for the future. Given the constantly changing social, economic, and political environment we face in public education, strategic planning becomes a necessity. In others areas, professional and even personal, we would not deny the import of planning, but when it comes to our work in schools, such systematic, thoughtful, and purposeful strategizing is imperative. If we are committed to improving student achievement as much as we say we are, then strategic leadership is a responsibility, even more, an obligation we cannot eschew.

As we close this book on strategic leadership, it is important to underscore a caveat implied, if not stated more explicitly, throughout our discussion. You should not assume that planning is a neat, linear process that occurs by simply setting goals and going about accomplishing them. Think for a moment how difficult it is to plan with accuracy one's own future, and then imagine trying to do likewise for scores of professionals and hundreds of students within the context of one school building. It's a challenging, if not impossible, task. Strategic planning should not be conceived as a restrictive, top-down, even perfunctory process. The process, as best practice, should be engaging, participatory, and developmental.

A fine line exists between planning as a management task and strategizing as a way of leading a school. Sergiovanni (2001) makes the point more precisely: "For linear conditions with tight structures, planning as traditionally conceived is a useful management *tactic* that can achieve the anticipated results, but as a *strategy*, traditional planning locks us into a course of action that often does not make sense once events are underway" (p. 58). Sergiovanni certainly acknowledges that under specific conditions or needs (e.g., establishing a financial

105

strategic plan; see Garner, 2004) where precision and clarity are necessary, effective managers do undertake detailed planning. However, under many other circumstances and needs, he points to an alternative way of addressing strategic planning. Conceiving the planning process as developmental, nonlinear, and loosely structured makes sense. He says, "It makes managerial sense to allow people to make decisions in ways that make sense to them providing that the decisions they make embody shared values and commitments" (p. 59). His alternative embodies four ideas, if not steps (pp. 58–59):

- Be clear about basic directions (set the tone and charter the mission).
- Provide purpose and build a shared covenant. (What are our shared goals, values, and operating principles?)
- Practice tight and loose management (hold people accountable to shared values, but provide them with empowerment and enablement to decide what to do, when, and how).
- Evaluate processes and outcomes (be sure that decisions and events embody shared values).

Strategic planning therefore incorporates both traditional and alternative conceptions or processes. Effective principals manage and lead for strategic leadership, because we share with our school colleagues an abiding commitment to educational excellence for all people, especially our major clients, our students.

Resource A

Realities of Strategic Leadership:
In-Basket Simulations

T his section highlights some of the realities of school-community leadership using an approach called "In-Basket Simulations." It is a study technique derived from an approach used when I studied for licensure as a principal in New York City. The approach was developed by the Institute for Research and Professional Development (http://www.nycenet.edu/opm/opm/profservices/rfp1b723.html). Scenarios that you as a principal might encounter are presented for your reaction. For instance, "A letter from an irate parent complaining that her child is intentionally being ignored during instruction in class by the teacher is sent to your attention. What would you do?" Challenging you to confront real-life phenomena under controlled conditions, these simulated in-basket items will prompt critical inquiry.

Here are suggestions to guide you as you complete these in-basket exercises:

1. Think and respond as if you are a principal, not a teacher or an assistant principal.

2. Place yourself mentally in each situation as if the case were actually happening to you.

3. Draw on your experiences and from what you've learned from others. Think of a principal you respect, and ask yourself, "What would Mr. or Ms. X have done?"

4. Make distinctions between actions you would personally take and actions you would delegate to others.

5. Utilize resources (personnel or otherwise) to assist you.

6. Think about your response, and then share it with a colleague for her or his reaction.

7. Record your response, and then a day later reread the scenario and your response. Would you still have reacted the same way?

During an interview, you are asked to respond to the following scenarios or questions:

- You are a newly assigned principal to an urban high school in which strategic planning has never been adopted. You intend to develop such a plan. Describe the steps you'd take to initiate, implement, and monitor the plan.

- As a new principal in a suburban middle school, you share your vision for inclusive practice to the faculty. Most faculty members are tenured, with an average of 14 years' teaching experience. You find few volunteers for your goal-setting committee. You surmise that teachers are resisting your emphasis on inclusion. One teacher tells you point-blank, "We don't want special ed kids included in our classes full time. We have enough classroom management problems without having to add these other 'needy' kids." How do you react to such resistance to your ideas?

- You cannot find any volunteers to join the action research committee designed to undertake a needs assessment that will form the basis for your strategic plan. What do you do?

- As elementary school principal in a suburban neighborhood with limited financial and material resources, you find that you must prioritize the numerous proposals requesting funds. You decide to fund the school trip committee's proposal but turn down the request from the textbook committee. Jim, a tenured faculty member who chairs the committee, demands an explanation why his proposal was rejected. Before letting you respond, he states emphatically, "If my committee's proposal is not funded, the fifth-grade teachers will no longer participate in the strategic plan initiative." Your response?

- Would you write the strategic plan by yourself? Explain why or why not.

- As a high school principal, you inform the English department that, according to data collected over the past semester, students are not making adequate progress academically. You request a plan from the department to raise student achievement. The department chair-person responds to your request by claiming that the data used were erroneous. "In fact," he says, "students according to our internal data are performing quite well." How would you respond?

- As a brand-new principal in your first day on the job in an urban high school, you are challenged by the fact that the school has a long history of inadequate leadership (six principals over a three-year period) and a faculty whose members quarrel frequently, rarely social-ize with each other, and contend with each other for scarce resources. You want to undertake a SWOT analysis and then act on a strategic plan to help mend wounds and rally faculty around a common vision and mission. Describe your actions in detail. How do politics affect your work, and how would you overcome your political challenges?

- Your middle school is riddled with high teacher turnover, partly because the school is located in a low-socioeconomic-status part of town. More than 95% of students in your school receive free lunch. Teachers work in isolation of each other and rarely, if ever, meet to dis-cuss instructional or curricular issues. Your two assistant principals don't like each other and are not very hard workers. You surmise they are burnt out. Parent involvement is negligible, and teacher and staff morale is low. You want to transform this school into a model school for the district and even the state. You are highly energetic and enthusiastic. As a people-oriented leader and new to the school (recently transferred from another school in the district), you know much about transforma-tional leadership. How would you go about building leadership capacity and sustainability in this school? Describe your actions in detail.

- You are a newly assigned principal to an elementary school, and you are interested in undertaking a needs assessment. You want to sur-vey how staff, parents, and students feel about the effectiveness of the school's goals in three areas: curriculum, organization, and school cli-mate. Your questionnaire should include items about academic goals, monitoring of student progress, teacher effectiveness, administrative leadership, rewards and incentives for students, order and discipline, parent and community involvement, and so forth. Describe how you would use these results to improve your school, paying particular atten-tion to student achievement.

- You have implemented a new literacy-based reading program in your middle school. How would you go about assessing its effectiveness?

- You want to transform your school, but "politics" seems to be getting in the way. Identify three primary political obstacles and how you would go about dealing with them in order to effectively pursue your goal of transformational leadership.

- What are the connections among strategic planning, data-driven decision making, and transformational leadership?

Resource B

Assessing Your Role in Strategic Leadership

We would never recommend that a teacher walk into the classroom without adequate planning. Similarly, we would not be surprised that corporate executives plan strategically. As principal, you realize that purposeful and strategic planning is essential to your school's success. Some principals might complain that such detailed planning is too time-consuming and even unnecessary. Parenthetically, I have always been suspicious of some experienced teachers who report that they need not plan any more given their many years of experience. Most principals and teachers believe, however, that planning is critical to promoting student achievement. Strategic planning, of course, is very different from and much more complicated than teacher planning in a single classroom. Principals certainly realize that strategic planning involves deep reflection, visioning, goal setting, strategy development, wide collaboration, strategic thinking and action, and circumspect follow-through. These forward-thinking principals are willing to do anything they can to promote student learning. Strategic planning, they know, is an invaluable means and opportunity to help them achieve their goal. Involving all stakeholders in a school building to work toward some common goals and objectives and go about achieving them strategically is considered best practice in school administration. Please complete this questionnaire as a means of self-reflection or analysis in order to assess the extent to which you share this belief or passion about strategic planning. You realize, of course, that the survey is not scientific, and results therefore should be studied in that light. Please note that your responses are private. Your honest responses to the various items will serve as reflective tools to assist you in becoming an even better strategic leader.

SA = Strongly Agree ("For the most part, yes.")
 A = Agree ("Yes, but . . .")
 D = Disagree ("No, but . . .")
SD = Strongly Disagree ("For the most part, no.")

SA A D SD   1. I believe that strategic planning is well worth the effort and time it takes.

SA A D SD   2. I possess the knowledge necessary to implement a strategic plan.

SA A D SD   3. A well-designed strategic plan can make a big difference in my effectiveness as principal.

SA A D SD   4. I am committed to following through on my school's strategic plan.

SA A D SD   5. I will allocate sufficient funds to ensure that strategic goals are achieved.

SA A D SD   6. I am the most critical element that determines success of the strategic plan.

SA A D SD   7. My faculty and district colleagues support my vision of excellence for all students.

SA A D SD   8. Strategic planning is only as important as the goal of promoting high achievement for all students.

SA A D SD   9. I solicit input from internal and external stakeholders for my school's strategic plan.

SA A D SD 10. I would solicit assistance of outside consultants to help frame the strategic plan.

SA A D SD 11. I can articulate the relationship between strategic planning and high student achievement.

SA A D SD 12. I revisit the strategic plan on a yearly basis.

SA A D SD 13. The process of strategic planning is more important than the plan itself.

SA A D SD 14. There's no one best plan—I continually reflect, discuss, and revise portions of the plan to meet current and future needs.

SA A D SD 15. Strategic planning is an incremental, gradual process that does not provide panaceas for the work we do in schools.

SA A D SD 16. I see my role as advocate and facilitator in the strategic planning process.

SA A D SD 17. I discuss the strategic plan constantly in various forums and meetings.

SA A D SD 18. Teacher involvement and leadership are critical to the plan's success.

SA A D SD 19. I continually consult with my superintendent for support and input related to the school's strategic plan.

SA A D SD 20. I invite suggestions and constructive criticisms at all phases in the strategic planning process.

SA A D SD 21. Beyond the initial stages, the principal need not be directly involved in the strategic planning process, as long as someone is designated to be in charge.

SA A D SD 22. Effective strategic leaders encourage everyone in the school building to participate in the strategic planning process.

SA A D SD 23. Division of responsibilities for carrying out the strategic plan should be open, flexible, and on a volunteer basis, without designating or identifying specific individuals to take responsibility for certain areas.

SA A D SD 24. There's no need to involve school board members in the strategic planning process.

SA A D SD 25. Strategic planning committees should always meet often.

SA A D SD 26. Establishing specific timelines is inadvisable because it is so restrictive.

SA A D SD 27. The strategic planning process should be monitored by anyone who shows interest in doing so.

SA A D SD 28. Strategic planning is likely to be short term.

SA A D SD 29. I try to minimize politics in the strategic planning process.

SA A D SD 30. As strategic leader, I will take any action to ensure success.

Analyze your responses:

The first 20 statements reflect best practice. Each of the last 10 statements is inaccurate in some way. Can you identify the shortcoming in each statement, 21 through 30?

Resource C

An Annotated Bibliography of Best Resources

The literature on the principalship and related areas is extensive. The list below is not meant to serve as a comprehensive resource by any means. The selected titles I have annotated are few, but in my opinion, they are among the most useful references on the subject. Rather than "impress" you with a more extensive list, I have selected these outstanding works related to strategic leadership that will supplement my book quite well. I may have missed, of course, other important works. Nevertheless, the list below is a good start. Don't forget that life is a long journey of continuous learning. Continue to hone your skills by reading good books and journal articles on strategic leadership. No one is ever perfect, and everyone can learn something new by keeping current with the literature in the field. Share your readings and reactions with a colleague.

Data-Driven Decision Making

Holcomb, E. L. (2004). *Getting excited about data: Combining people, passion, and proof to maximize student achievement* (2nd ed.). Thousand Oaks, CA: Corwin.

Reader-friendly, practical, and content strong, this work enhances your work as strategic leader because it provides the skills necessary to make more effective decisions.

Streifer, P. A. (2004). *Tools and techniques for effective data-driven decision making.* Lanham, MD: ScarecrowEducation.

Provides a very useful and comprehensive understanding of the topic that addresses issues of leadership, policy development, and accountability. The case study approach makes this quick read very user-friendly.

Micropolitical Leadership

Black, J. A., & English, F. W. (1997). *What they don't tell you in schools of education about school administration.* Lancaster, PA: Technomic.

One of my favorite books, a must-read. Enjoyable, humorous, and packed with practical information, this work gives you insights into the realities of school politics you won't learn elsewhere. A classic that, in my estimation, should be reworked, updated, and republished.

Bolman, L. G., & Deal, T. E. (1997). *Reframing organizations: Artistry, choice, and leadership.* San Francisco: Jossey-Bass.

Bolman and Deal's "political frame" of leadership is a classic in the field. Familiarize yourself with their model, because it will provide you with insights to serve as a better strategic leader.

Freire, P. (1984). *The politics of education: Culture, power and liberation.* Westport, CT: Bergin & Garvey.

Someone once told me that the only way to learn about politics is to experience and learn from it. Although probably good advice, read this classic, which serves as a manifesto of sorts on the subject.

Spring, J. (2004). *Conflict of interests: The politics of American education.* New York: McGraw-Hill.

A comprehensive overview of politics in education from a historical perspective, this book serves as a foundation for current practice.

Strategic Leadership

Allison, M., & Kaye, J. (1997). *Strategic planning for nonprofit organizations: A practical guide and workbook.* New York: John Wiley & Sons.

Although not about education and schools specifically, this work is filled with practical advice that can easily be adapted to your work. Sometimes hearing a perspective from another field can serve to catapult a strategic effort.

Below, P. J., Morrisey, G. L., & Acomb, B. L. (1987). *The executive guide to strategic planning.* San Francisco: Jossey-Bass.

Offers a comprehensive approach to strategic planning: how to formulate strategic plans that will develop the school's strengths; be responsive to changing social, political, and economic conditions; and so on. Provides numerous charts, worksheets, and other resources.

Drucker, P. (1998). *The Drucker foundation self-assessment tool: Participant's workbook.* San Francisco: Drucker Foundation and Jossey-Bass.

Easy-to-read guide with practical and proven strategies for developing and sustaining a strategic plan.

Garner, C. W. (2004). *Education finance for school leaders: Strategic planning and administration.* Columbus, OH: Merrill/Prentice Hall.

Practical, and easy to use for a textbook.

Marazza, L. L. (2003). *The 5 essentials of organizational excellence: Maximizing schoolwide student achievement and performance.* Thousand Oaks, CA: Corwin.

Written by a school superintendent, this useful volume contains many insights and practical suggestions for strategic planning. It's not often one reads a book that hits the nail on the proverbial head—this one does.

Mintzberg, H. (1994). *The rise and fall of strategic planning.* New York: Free Press.

Provides a comprehensive background to the topic, reviews the extensive research in the field, and offers suggestions for planning and implementing strategic leadership. Scholarly, yet highly readable.

Web Resources on Strategic Leadership

http://www.allianceonline.org—The Alliance for Nonprofit Management, according to the Web site, "is the professional association of individuals and organizations devoted to improving the management and governance capacity of nonprofits—to assist nonprofits in fulfilling their mission." Although not directly discussing schools, this resource nevertheless offers many insights and practical suggestions.

http://www.consco.com—The Conservation Company offers varied tools and strategies for understanding and implementing strategic planning. Again, although not solely from a school's perspective, you can gain much information from this site.

http://www.mapnp.org/library/plan_dec/str_plan/str_plan.htm—The Free Management Library is one of the most comprehensive sites, detailing numerous aspects of strategic planning. Filled with useful information that you can relate to as principal.

Transformational Leadership

Bass, B. M., & Avolio, B. J. (Eds.). (1993). *Improving organizational effectiveness through transformational leadership.* Thousand Oaks, CA: Sage.

Well-written, thorough, and informative, this useful text is at once scholarly and practically relevant. Anyone interested in transforming a school should read this book.

Burns, J. M. (1982). *Leadership.* New York: Perennial.

A classic in the field of leadership, although not reader-friendly. Written for the scholar who wants to glean theoretical gems about leadership. Don't expect to walk away from this read with concrete strategies, but do expect a thorough, sensible, and deep knowledge of the subject. Although I would not recommend New York City Mayor Giuliani's book of the same title (because it depicts leadership in a narrow way), I would heartily recommend the Burns book, because it covers the topic with depth and breadth. Also, see his more recent *Transforming Leadership: The Pursuit of Happiness* (2003).

Fullan, M. (2003). *The moral imperative of school leadership.* Thousand Oaks, CA: Corwin.

A short must-read that will not only inspire but also provide you with leadership insights by one of the foremost scholars in the field.

Johnson, S., & Blanchard, K. H. (1998). *Who moved my cheese? An amazing way to deal with change in your work and in your life.* New York: G. P. Putnam's Sons.

Immensely popular, brief, and an easy read, this volume is light reading that can serve to inspire you. A good break from the more "scholarly"-type books out there.

Starratt, R. J. (1995). *Leaders with vision: The quest for school renewal.* Thousand Oaks, CA: Corwin.

Although difficult to read at times, this work is also a classic by a prominent scholar. Will help you ground your efforts at transformational leadership.

Web Resources on Organizational Change

http://www.hrdq.com—Organization Design and Development, Inc., whose mission, according to the Web site, is "to develop theory-based, results-driven training solutions that help organizations maximize the potential of their human resources." Founded in 1977, HRDQ offers you varied leadership resources that can enhance your role as strategic leader. Available are a free catalog, an e-newsletter, programs and workshops, assessment instruments, and so forth.

http://www.hayresourcesdirect.haygroup.com/—The Hay Group, Inc., is an organizational and human resources consulting firm. It provides, according to its Web site, "research-based, practical, and affordable assessment and development products." The resources provided by the Hay Group are among the most sophisticated resources on organizational leadership and are very useful in facilitating organizational change and much more.

Journals, Handbook, and Newspaper

Because this is the last volume in this seven-book series on the principalship, allow me to suggest several journal publications you should order and read on a continuous basis. These journals provide you with the most current research and perspectives in the field and should be part of your professional literature. Strategic leaders, especially, remain cognizant of what other scholars and practitioners have to say about leadership and related areas. One essential newspaper is also highly recommended reading.

Journals

American School Board Journal—Visit http://www.asbj.com for details.

Education and Urban Society—Visit http://www.corwinpress.com for details.

Educational Administration Abstracts—Provides abstract reviews of key articles from various journals. Visit http://www.corwinpress.com for details.

Educational Administration Quarterly—Visit http://www.corwinpress.com for details.

Educational Leadership—Visit http://www.ascd.org for details.

Educational Management Administration and Leadership—Visit http://www.corwinpress.com for details.

Journal of School Leadership—Visit http://www.scarecroweducation.com for details.

Kappan—Visit http://www.pdkintl.org for details.

NASSP Bulletin—Visit http://www.nassp.org for details.

Principal—Visit http://www.naesp.org for details.

Principal Leadership—Visit http://www.nassp.org for details.

The Education Digest—Provides condensed versions of previously published articles from various relevant publications. Visit http://www.eddigest.com for details.

Handbook

English, F. W. (Ed.). (2004). *The Sage handbook of educational leadership.* Thousand Oaks, CA: Sage.

Newspaper

Education Week—Visit http://www.edweek.org for details.

References

Alliance for Nonprofit Management. (2003–2004a). "The benefits of planning." Retrieved July 28, 2005, from http://www.allianceonline.org/FAQ/strategic_planning/what_do_i_need_to_know.faq

Alliance for Nonprofit Management. (2003–2004b). "Gathering perceptions about the organization." Retrieved July 28, 2005, from http://www.allianceonline.org/FAQ/strategic_planning/what_is_situation_assessment.faq

Alliance for Nonprofit Management. (2003–2004c). "Planning should be an inclusive process." Retrieved July 28, 2005, from http://www.allianceonline.org/FAQ/strategic_planning/what_are_individual_roles.faq

Bass, B. M. (1985). *Leadership and performance beyond expectations.* New York: Free Press.

Bass, B. M. (1997). Does the transactional/transformational leadership transcend organizational and national boundaries? *American Psychologist, 52,* 130–139.

Bennis, W. G., & Nanus, B. (1985). *Leaders: The strategies for taking charge.* New York: Harper & Row.

Bolman, L. G., & Deal, T. E. (1991). *Reframing organizations: Artistry, choice, and leadership* (2nd ed.). San Francisco: Jossey-Bass.

Bolman, L. G., & Deal, T. E. (1997). *Reframing organizations: Artistry, choice, and leadership.* San Francisco: Jossey-Bass.

Bryson, J. M. (1995). *Strategic planning for public and nonprofit organizations.* San Francisco: Jossey-Bass.

Bum, B., & Payment, M. (2000). *Assessments A to Z: Collection of 50 questionnaires, instruments, and inventories.* Port Chester, NY: National Professional Resources.

Burns, J. M. (1978). *Leadership.* New York: Harper & Row.

Cotton, K. (2003). *Principals and student achievement: What research says.* Alexandria, VA: Association for Supervision and Curriculum Development.

Cremin, L. A. (1966). *The genius of American education.* New York: Vintage.

Datnow, A. (2005). The sustainability of comprehensive school reform models in changing district and state contexts. *Educational Administration Quarterly, 41,* 121–153.

Davies, B. (Ed.). (2002). *The essentials of leadership.* London: Paul Chapman.

Davies, B., & Davies, B. J. (2005). Strategic leadership. In B. Davies (Ed.), *The essentials of school leadership* (pp. 10–30). Thousand Oaks, CA: Corwin.

Duffy, F. M. (1991). Q2—Power, politics, and ethics: The arena for effective leadership in higher education. *College and University Personnel Association Journal, 42*(3), 1–6.

Duffy, F. M. (2003). *Courage, passion, & vision: A guide to leading systemic school improvement.* Lanham, MD: Scarecrow Press.

Fink, A., & Kosecoff, J. (1998). *How to conduct surveys: A step-by-step guide* (2nd ed.). Thousand Oaks, CA: Sage.

Fullan, M. (2003a). *Change forces with a vengeance.* London: Routledge Falmer.

Fullan, M. (2003b). Implementing change at the building level. In W. A. Owings & L. S. Kaplan (Eds.), *Best practices, best thinking, and the emerging issues in school leadership* (pp. 31–36). Thousand Oaks, CA: Corwin.

Garner, C. W. (2004). *Education finance for school leaders: Strategic planning and administration.* Upper Saddle River, NJ: Pearson/Merrill Prentice Hall.

Gladwell, M. (2000). *The tipping point.* Boston: Little, Brown.

Glanz, J. (1991). *Bureaucracy and professionalism: The evolution of public school supervision.* Cranbury, NJ: Fairleigh Dickinson University Press.

Glanz, J. (2003). *Action research: An educational leader's guide to school improvement.* Norwood, MA: Christopher-Gordon.

Hansen, J. H., & Liftin, E. (1999). *Leadership for continuous school improvement.* Swampscott, MA: Watersun.

Hax, A. C., & Majluf, N. S. (1996). *The strategy concept and process: A pragmatic approach.* Upper Saddle River, NJ: Prentice Hall.

Heck, D. J., & Weiss, I. R. (2005). *Strategic leadership for education reform: Lessons from the statewide systemic initiatives program* (CPRE Policy Brief). Philadelphia: University of Pennsylvania Consortium for Policy Research in Education.

Heritage, M., & Chen, E. (2005). Why data skills matter in school improvement. *Phi Delta Kappan, 86,* 707–710.

Horsley, D. L., & Loucks-Horsley, S. (1998). CBAM brings order to the tornado of change. *Journal of Staff Development, 19*(4). Retrieved June 5, 2005, from http://www.nsdc.org/library/publications/jsd/horsley194.cfm

House, R. J. (1976). A theory of charismatic leadership. In J. G. Hunt & L. L. Larson (Eds.), *Leadership: The cutting edge* (pp. 189–207). Carbondale: Southern Illinois University Press.

Jones, J. (2005). *Management skills in schools: A resource for school leaders.* London: Paul Chapman.

Kaser, J., Mundry, S., Stiles, K. E., & Loucks-Horsley, S. (2002). *Leading every day: 124 actions for effective leadership.* Thousand Oaks, CA: Corwin.

Kerr, K. A., Marsh, J., & Ikemoto, G. S. (2005, April). *Districtwide strategies to promote data use for instructional improvement.* Paper presented at the Annual Meeting of the American Educational Research Association, Montreal, Quebec, Canada.

Krueger, R. A. (2000). *Focus groups: A practical guide for applied research* (3rd ed.). Thousand Oaks, CA: Sage.

Lambert, L. (1998). *Building leadership capacity in schools.* Alexandria, VA: Association for Supervision and Curriculum Development.

Leithwood, K., & Jantzi, D. (2005). Transformational leadership. In B. Davies (Ed.), *The essentials of school leadership* (pp. 31–43). Thousand Oaks, CA: Corwin.

Liedtka, J. M. (1998). Linking strategic thinking with strategic planning. *Strategy and Leadership, 26*(4), 30–35. Retrieved July 28, 2005, from http://www.swin.edu.au/corporate/spq/docs/prospect/FB4Jun2001.pdf

Litwin, M. S. (1995). *How to measure survey reliability and validity.* Thousand Oaks, CA: Sage.

Lunenburg, F. C., & Ornstein, A. C. (2004). *Educational administration: Concepts and practices* (4th ed.). Belmont, CA: Wadsworth.

Lyddon, J. W. (1999, April). *Strategic planning in smaller nonprofit organizations: A practical guide for the process.* Kalamazoo: Nonprofit Leadership and Administration Faculty, Western Michigan University. Retrieved July 28, 2005, from http://www.wmich.edu/nonprofit/Guide/guide7.htm

Marazza, L. L. (2003). *The 5 essentials of organizational excellence: Maximizing schoolwide student achievement and performance.* Thousand Oaks, CA: Corwin.

Marshall, C., & Rossman, G. B. (1999). *Designing qualitative research* (3rd ed.). Newbury Park, CA: Sage.

Matthews, L. J., & Crow, G. M. (2003). *Being and becoming a principal: Role conceptions for contemporary principals and assistant principals.* Boston: Allyn & Bacon.

McNamara, C. (1999). "Strategic planning (in nonprofit or for-profit organizations)." Retrieved July 31, 2005, from http://www.mapnp.org/library/plan_dec/str_plan/str_plan.htm

Mills, G. E. (2000). *Action research: A guide for the teacher researcher.* Upper Saddle River, NJ: Merrill.

Mintzberg, H. (1994). *The rise and fall of strategic planning.* New York: Free Press.

Mishler, E. G. (1986). *Research interviewing: Context and process.* Cambridge, MA: Harvard University Press.

Mittenthal, R. (2002). *Ten keys to successful strategic planning* [briefing paper]. Philadelphia: Conservation Company.

Nadelstern, E., Price, J. R., & Listhaus, A. (2000). Student empowerment through the professional development of teachers. In J. Glanz & L. Behar-Horenstein (Eds.), *Paradigm debates in curriculum and supervision: Modern and postmodern perspectives* (pp. 265–275). Westport, CT: Bergin & Garvey.

National Association of Secondary School Principals (NASSP). (1987). *Comprehensive assessment of school environments.* Reston, VA: Author.

Northouse, P. G. (2003). *Leadership: Theory and practice.* Thousand Oaks, CA: Sage.

Popham, W. J. (2001). *Classroom assessment: What teachers need to know.* Boston: Allyn & Bacon.

Ramsey, R. D. (2003). *School leadership from A to Z.* Thousand Oaks, CA: Corwin.

Robbins, P., & Alvy, H. B. (2003). *The principal's companion: Strategies and hints to make the job easier* (2nd ed.). Thousand Oaks, CA: Corwin.

Sanders, J. R. (2000). *Evaluating school programs: An educator's guide* (2nd ed.). Thousand Oaks, CA: Corwin.

Seidman, I. E. (1998). *Interviewing as qualitative research: A guide for researchers in education and the social sciences* (2nd ed.). New York: Teachers College Press.

Sergiovanni, T. J. (2001). *The principalship: A reflective practice perspective* (4th ed.). Boston: Allyn & Bacon.

Shaver, H. (2004). *Organize, communicate, empower: How principals can make time for leadership.* Thousand Oaks, CA: Corwin.

Starratt, R. J. (1995). *Leaders with vision: The quest for school renewal.* Thousand Oaks, CA: Corwin.

Sullivan, S., & Glanz, J. (2005). *Supervision that improves teaching: Strategies and techniques* (2nd ed.). Thousand Oaks, CA: Corwin.

Sullivan, S., & Glanz, J. (2006). *Building effective learning communities: Strategies for leadership, learning, & collaboration.* Thousand Oaks, CA: Corwin.

Thomas, S. J. (1999). *Designing surveys that work! A step-by-step guide.* Bloomington, IN: Phi Delta Kappa.

Tyack, D. B. (1974). *The one best system: A history of American public education.* Cambridge, MA: Harvard University Press.

Vaughn, S., Schumm, J. S., & Sinagub, J. M. (1996). *Focus group interviews in education and psychology.* Thousand Oaks, CA: Sage.

Wayman, J. C., Midgley, S., & Stringfield, S. (2005, April). *Collaborative teams to support data-based decision making and instructional improvement.* Paper presented at the Annual Meeting of the American Educational Research Association, Montreal, Quebec, Canada.

Weber, M. (1947). *The theory of social and economic organizations* (T. Parsons, Trans.). New York: Free Press.

West Morris Regional High School District. (2000–2005). *Long range plan.* Chester, NJ: Author.

Wholey, J. S., Hatry, H. P., & Newcomer, K. E. (1994). *Handbook of practical program evaluation.* San Francisco: Jossey-Bass.

Wilmore, E. L. (2002). *Principal leadership: Applying the new Educational Leadership Constituent Council (ELCC) standards.* Thousand Oaks, CA: Corwin.

Young, P. G. (2004). *You have to go to school—You're the principal: 101 tips to make it better for your students, your staff, and yourself.* Thousand Oaks, CA: Corwin.

Young, V. M. (2005, April). *Data-driven instruction: Building a practice-based theory.* Paper presented at the Annual Meeting of the American Educational Research Association, Montreal, Quebec, Canada.

Index

Note: Page numbers with an *f* are figures; those with a *t* are tables.

**CORWIN
PRESS**

The Corwin Press logo—a raven striding across an open book—represents the union of courage and learning. Corwin Press is committed to improving education for all learners by publishing books and other professional development resources for those serving the field of PreK–12 education. By providing practical, hands-on materials, Corwin Press continues to carry out the promise of its motto: **"Helping Educators Do Their Work Better."**